SUCCESS

EXPRESS LANE

YOUR ROADMAP

TO

PERSONAL ACHIEVEMENT

James Taiwo

Library of Congress Control Number: **2018907825**

LLCN Imprint Name: **Queens, New York**

ISBN-13: **978-1-7325213-1-5**

Acknowledgement

To Funmi Taiwo:

Thank you for being a supportive wife and especially for your relentless encouragement to make this dream a reality.

Table of Contents

Introduction

The importance of success cannot be overstated. A whole lifetime dedicated to its teaching is entirely worth the effort. "Success" is a hot topic that lingers on nearly everyone's lips due to the crucial part it plays in life. Most people, when asked, will answer in the affirmative about the desire for and pursuit of success. Few people have planned or want to live a life of impoverishment and suffering, or to exist without making any significant impact on the world. The general wish is to have the means to live comfortably, provide for our families, and be relevant in a positive way. Being remembered long after we are gone would be a nice bonus.

Perhaps much more than other generation, Millennials pursue success with a feverish enthusiasm. They have an avid interest in it, akin to a quest. Unfortunately, despite the existence of the desire for this crucial element, many people do not have the necessary understanding of what success is or how to attain it. They are in the dark about what it is and what it is not, what to do and what not to do to become a success-minded individual. Some of those who do know what it is are not ready to pay the price for it. Success is not an abstract concept put together by an intellectual character. Success is neither magical nor sudden. It is not an instantaneous event. It does not occur independently of other factors. Rather, it is an accumulation of several elements that must be considered by consciously taking steps in a particular direction.

The Success Express Lane was created to make success as real and practical as it can be. From real-life stories to a delineation of concrete steps, you will have a comprehensive breakdown of what success is, what it entails, and how to achieve it. Enough with the abstract! Let's get down to the facts and do away with the mentality of poverty.

Find yourself a comfortable seat in a place devoid of disturbances and unwanted distractions, delve into the honey pot of a life-changing mentality, and enjoy every step along the way.

IT STARTS WITH THE MIND

... if it can be thought, it can be done, a problem can be overcome

E.A. Bucchianeri

John and Tyler are both Sales Executives with the aspiration of becoming the next Vice President of their company. Both men are hardworking and up and coming in their profession. However, while John believes nothing could stand in his way to sitting in the chair, Tyler is of the opinion that only a better-qualified person could be elected. He often tells John the same thing, but the latter never agrees to such submissions. He would become the Vice President because he could. He does not believe in the traditions from which Tyler reaches his conclusions. John would be the first person to break free from the shackles of such holdings. One year down the lane, Tyler is still a Sales Executive while John has risen through the ranks in the fastest way. Everyone is surprised at the speed with which he climbed. It had never worked that way before.

What happened?

John rose through the ranks in his mind long before it ever materialized in reality. The mind is the seat of all innovations. Whatever you set your mind on, it is just a matter of time before you find yourself accomplishing it. If you perceive yourself as a failure, you will soon start exhibiting such tendencies and characteristics. Stop labeling yourself as what you are not.

3

You have been configured for success. You have its DNA swimming in your body, and it is your job to tap into the abundance of resources flowing in your mind. Train yourself always to think positively about yourself. No one can determine your success but you. Whether you will become a name on everyone's lips can only be determined by you. You are the only person who can get in the way of your success. People may say whatever they wish, but if you do not agree, their negative statement will wash off without leaving any stain on you.

You may have heard similar ideas before, but this book contains concrete steps to make them a reality. It takes active work for you to be able to attain this level of positive-mindedness, but it is infinitely attainable.

> *You are the only person who can get in the way of your success.*

THE STAKE OF SUCCESS

We are all born ignorant, but one must work hard to remain stupid.

Benjamin Franklin

Success stories can never be completed without the mention of some notable names in history. While we do not want to replicate the lives of these successful people, there are always lessons to be learned from them. Benjamin Franklin was a man renowned for his significant contributions to science, the arts, and even politics. Although he never was elected to a high office of the United States, Franklin did play a significant role as one of the country's founding fathers. Franklin drafted the Constitution and the Declaration of Independence, and he was also very much involved in the negotiation of the 1783 Treaty of Paris, which led to the eventual end of the Revolutionary War. Franklin had many accolades to his name; some of his innovations include the Franklin stove, the flexible catheter, bifocals, the American penny, the Armonica, and the rocking chair.

Franklin, like many other successful men, did not start with much Born to a soap and candle maker, he was the youngest of his father's children—the fifteenth. However, the young man's intelligence shone through at a very early age. Life landed a blow against young Franklin; although he could read a very young age, he had to stop school at the age of ten to begin an apprenticeship with his brother to help support the family. It was a difficult time, but he used the situation to his advantage. He acquired the skill of newspaper publishing, which he later utilized to a large extent. Franklin developed an interest in politics and wrote extensively about it, but his writings never saw the light of the day at his brother James' publishing house, so sixteen-year-old Franklin adopted the pen name of Mrs. Silence Dogood. With this, he was able to excite his readers with about fourteen of his essays. As expected, an end came to the publication of the political pieces when his brother got wind of their sources.

At the age of seventeen, Franklin took charge of his life and left for Philadelphia, which was the beginning of his journey to greatness. The son of a candle and soap maker did not end up as a nobody, because he understood the stake of success. He did not even complete his formal education, but that was not a deterrent. There are tons of lessons to be learned from such a brave and determined heart.

Every human being is given an equal opportunity to go through three critical phases in life development. It does not matter if the stages are presented on a silver platter or a wooden tray. Sequentially, one stage precedes the other. The stages roll into one another to form a natural growth. As such, man is made to navigate through the constant and inevitable phases of childhood, youth and adulthood. They are unavoidable, except the growth and development of the individual are not completely preordained. Contrary to what many people think or assume, the growth process that brings an increase in physical stature is not automatically complemented with intellectual maturity. It is entirely possible for a person to be fully developed physically without equal accompanying mental and emotional growth. In the same vein, intellectual maturity can also be achieved without the physical development of the body. It takes the infusion of a conscious effort to have an accompanying and equal intellectual growth as the physical development of the body occurs. Franklin was just sixteen years old when he made the significant decision to use a pseudonym to evade his brother's eagle-sharp eyes and equally determined mind. He was still a minor by law when he decided to change the course of his life forever.

A person who desires success must take the journey of personal development to improve his or her intellectual base and make it perform at its full threshold. He or she may have the resource of a natural intellect, but it

> *Every human being is given an equal opportunity to go through three critical phases in life development. It does not matter if the stages are presented on a silver platter or a wooden tray.*

will not operate at its full potential until an external force is put in place. The person will have to pull his or her treasures out of the pile of rubles and brush off some dirt before his or her mind can fully function to earn great success. He or she has got some job to do!

Success does not occur suddenly. It is not one of the instantaneous incidents of life. It is subject to different laws and principles. Many people are unfortunately unaware of this piece of information. A person who wants to achieve life success cannot be someone that folds his hands and expects magic of success to happen! He cannot wait around to let life dictate situations as it desires. If nature is given the opportunity to become the sole driver of what takes place, the result is an undesirous life without control. A success admirer must be ready to shoulder the responsibility of tasking himself to excel beyond mediocrity. His thought patterns and mode of operations cannot be the same as others'. There must be a distinguishing factor, one that sets him apart from other people.

Arrays of information abound on the peculiar traits of highly successful people. He must be sitting in the driver's seat to steer the win of success to his advantage. To make this happen, he has to have a dream and be creative in making it happen. That is, he must bring the end goal into perspective as he embarks on his success journey.

However, some people misconceive the factors that lead to success generation. They focus on education as if it's the only contributor to success; whereas many more factors are involved. Education alone does not amount to success; it plays a major role, but it's just not enough on its own. A person does need focused education to make a tangible dent in his quest for success. Focused education goes beyond book knowledge; it incorporates knowledge with practical ideas and implementation to help a person have the tenacity to have success and keep it.

Education aside, a person who desires success must be sure to understand the principles of success and live by them. He needs discipline to meet the standard. Discipline will help him stay within the success lane to achieve an expected result. Discipline will help him thrive while others are failing. Meanwhile, the scope of achieving success will be limited for a person who lacks discipline. The stake of grasping success will be too high for him, even when he sees success at his horizon. An undisciplined person will always be one step away from achieving greater success unless he breaks away from his routine.

There is no substitute for knowledge and discipline on the success roadmap! Anyone who has these two virtues will earn himself the ability to keep driving his aspiration. He will even have the tenacity to weather unfriendly circumstances and still thrive. Better still, he will be able to reach beyond his competitors.

The Quest for Success

The pursuit of success is personal, and someone who takes the journey must not be obliged to do so under duress. Success exploration must be perceived as a voluntary course. No one should feel coerced to embark on a journey that will improve his or her life. That is, an individual has the freedom to either pursue the success roadmap or reject it. However, it is advisable that someone who for any reason refuses the idea of success pursuit still learns what it takes to be successful. Perhaps the person will consider reversing his decision once he knows what is at stake for him.

Someone who makes a personal choice to pursue success ought to do so with all seriousness. He needs to steer clear of mediocre lifestyle. He has to be a person who plans and works hard to bring his goal to the highest peak achievable. The person must understand the importance of the practical implementation of a dream. It does not end with just appreciation or knowing; he must be ready to subject his vision to it. At every point, he should be prepared to bring his goal to reality. He should know that people are only interested in sharing their hard-earned money for what they can see has benefits for them. They will not reward him for what he conceives in his mind, no matter how beautiful it is! No one makes deals with dreams, but everyone loves tangible achievement.

Goal implementation is far better than nursing a dream. Someone who makes an effort to bring his vision to the stage of practical implementation will earn some benefits for himself. He will have some opportunities that may never have been available had the dream remained in the corner of his mind. Not only will people reward him for what they can see and benefit from, but practical implementation will also help him to make prospective decisions that will earn him more benefits. A person who brings his dream to a realistic sense will have the advantage of tweaking it for improvement. He will understand what is feasible and practical. That is the only time he can exert any influence.

An individual who brings his dream to the stage of practical implementation can learn about the odds involved. He can either solve or navigate around them. He can even wholly eradicate a work when he feels the odds are higher than the prospects involved. That is, the

> *No one makes deals with dreams, but everyone loves tangible achievement.*

dream implementer can make a proper evaluation of his work to determine whether the work is worth pursuing or not. He also has the advantage of tailoring it to fit the success he envisaged.

Goal planning and adept implementation are two critical factors of success generation. Someone can consider them as the belly of a fish where all goodies lie. A person who admires success must put planning into perspective; he cannot *mumble jumble* his tasks and expect them to lead to astounding success. He must set his goals, plan and implement them appropriately. The plan must be formidable enough to allow his work to have a smooth run from start to finish.

Indeed, *anything worth doing at all is worth doing well*; a person who wants to embark on a successful journey ought to subject his work to a few litmus tests to determine if his goal is worth pursuing or not. He must take this step to save himself from any aggravation that may later develop as he advances in the implementation process. If he concludes that his goal has no substantial benefit, then he has no business pursuing it. He should drop it and use the energy on something else that has promise. Even when a goal is considered to have possibilities, the person still must evaluate further and determine the strength of the success. He must analyze and decide if it will be durable enough to weather any unanticipated circumstance that may arise.

Following the rule of the *status quo* does not work when attempting to create groundbreaking success. A person who wants to stand out from the majority must be someone who avoids redundant routines that have earned other people limited success. A success admirer must venture to think and operate differently if he wants to stand out from others. He cannot approach his business similarly to what others have and still expect to have groundbreaking success. The mathematics will not add up. The rule of thumb requires him not to share a typical attitude with others if he wants to dominate them. He must tweak his thought pattern and

> *Following the rule of the status quo does not work when attempting to create groundbreaking success.*

have an unusual approach to his work so that he can stand out from the crowd. He must also be creative and make his innovation stand out.

Key Points

➢ Everybody must go through three specific and constant phases of development in life: childhood, youth, and adulthood.

➢ Physical development does not necessarily mean an accompanying intellectual growth. Each can occur without the other.

➢ Success is not instantaneous.

➢ Education is not equivalent to success, and it does not make anyone successful. It will only provide an excellent platform for success to happen.

➢ Discipline will help you stay on course.

➢ The pursuit of success is personal.

➢ Do not simply dream; act on your dream.

WHAT IS SUCCESS?

*To live the lives we truly want and deserve, and
not just the lives we settle for, we need a Third
Metric, a third measure of success that goes
beyond the two metrics of money and power, and
consists of four pillars: well-being, wisdom,
wonder, and giving.*

Ariana Huffington

Jane and Linda are two friends, but their lives are different. Jane is a scientist who loves to learn new things, and every day she sits behind the microscope to discover them. Research and development are two words in her vocabulary that she takes very seriously. Although she has made no ground-breaking discovery, she has made some contributions. She has a few awards to her name, but she is not rich. She lives a comfortable life and loves what she is doing. She is happy to influence and develop the standards of living of the masses by improving healthcare services, even if it is in somewhat insignificant proportions.

Linda, on the other hand, is a business mogul. Unlike her friend, she is always in the news for one reason or another. She was featured on an NBC show as one of the most influential entrepreneurs of the year. Her name is fast becoming a household one. Everyone likes to associate with her and would do anything to get the tiniest fraction of her time.

An average person will conclude that Linda is more successful than Jane, which brings to the mind the question of the nature of success. At the end of this chapter, I will ask what success is, and I hope the answer will be clear.

The word success is more or less a universal term that is used to describe achievement. It could be a position, intelligence, innovation, money (de-emphasized), and many other things. However, most people misunderstand the meaning of the word, as they limit its definition to money acquisition. They believe the more money a person has, the more successful he has become. This thought is far from the truth. Money is never equivalent to success, although it may come with it. Other important factors are needed to drive the definition of success home. Any comprehensive definition of success must be inclusive of the terms "satisfaction" and "sustainability." Merriam-Webster is credited with defining success as a "favorable or desired outcome." This definition can be further explained as "a satisfying by-product of an exercise performed." That is, a person who performs a task must derive satisfaction from any end product he receives before he can declare it as successful. From the brief illustration, Jane was not wealthy in monetary terms, but she enjoyed what she did. She could go on and on about it even if she got no reward of any kind. In the context of the **Success Express Lane**, to be declared "successful," an endeavor must have the following three essential elements:

- [ ] It must create a by-product

- [ ] It must bring satisfaction

- [ ] It must be sustainable

An achievement declared as successful must not be constricted to cash value. This mentality needs to become renewed for the success-conscious individual. success must create a satisfying product that has added security. That is, it must be durable enough to pass the test of time. There should be a remembrance that you "did this thing" or "created that stuff" from generation to generation. In music, ever-green songs exist; they are such that have been found to stand the test of time in the sense that no matter the characteristic feature of a particular generation and its peculiar likes, people would always love and sing such a song.

Success has three crucial stages that chronologically overlay each other to generate the desired end-product: *inception, maturation,* and *completion.* Each stage slowly rolls into the other, just like the stages of physical development discussed earlier, until a vivid outcome is realized. A person must understand how each of the steps can lead to his prospect. Inadequate knowledge of the stages will increase his chances of making an erratic decision that can affect his success attempt.

> *A successful endeavor must have the following three essential elements:*
>
> ☐ It must create a by-product
> ☐ It must bring satisfaction
> ☐ It must be sustainable

People who are quick to label whatever glows as successful are mostly folks who have limited knowledge of what success is about or what it entails. They tend to make erratic decisions that can disrupt the progress of their work. These folks are prone to acting in a manner contrary to how they should. They throw a party and celebrate their intangible achievement when they ought to roll up their sleeves and seize the moment to make their work have a breakthrough.

Inexperienced folks naively interrupt the flow of their work process; they celebrate their little achievement not realizing that their

15

behavior has just caused them the loss of a better opportunity en-route. Sometimes these folks do not even know what they have lost until the opportunity is no longer available. Meanwhile, a prospecting person will take caution and make a careful evaluation of his work. He will not be quick to declare an achievement as successful until he has scrutinized it to determine that it meets the standards of satisfaction and sustainability. What advantage does a product have that cannot pass the test of time? It blooms today but fails in a few days or a few months. A prospecting person will ensure his work can weather a few intermittent interruptions before he declares it as successful.

Now, if I may dare ask, do you now know what success is and what it is not?

The Reality: The State of Success

Success tosses the world around and divides people into the category of folks who are successful and those who are not. Success also draws a fine line for those who are wealthy but are not successful; those who find themselves sitting on the fence are individuals who cannot account for their wealth. They are criminals who exploited other people for their benefits. They may regard themselves as successful, but they are far away from being so, because they constantly violate the principles of success!

The cruel wealthy do not earn the honor of being referred to as successful people. They exploit the system that ought to benefit the majority, thereby widening the gap of separation between the rich and the poor. Those wealthy nuisances exist in every society; they have similar patterns of operation, which are to exploit and oppress disadvantaged people.

The so-called elites have turned themselves to demigods in some unlawful countries, and they have wiped out the middle-class economy. These cronies have control of their society, and they can influence the government to their advantage. Mention any sector; the cronies are there. They are in control of finance, education, health, justice. The cruel rich have turned the tables around to their advantage and forced impoverished people to a disadvantaged edge. In this manner, the poor get poorer while the rich get richer than ever.

Dirty politics have plagued third world countries, thereby making it difficult for ordinary citizens to survive. So-called democracy is packed full of corruption. Jobs are scarce, and leaders have no plan to address the situation, indicating the worst is yet to happen! An educated person rarely finds a job related to his field of study. An average university graduate will prefer instead to take any available position than to stay idle and become a nuisance. Meanwhile, the lack of jobs has made many people who have bright minds give up their job search leaving an incredible effect on their national economy. What a pity in the *nations of no future.*

Third-world countries are not only to be blamed for wealth inequality; both the first- and second-world nations share equal blame. The so-called advanced nations have systems that favor the rich at the expense of the poor. Take, for example, that tertiary education is far more expensive in the United States than in many other countries. Only a handful of people can pay out-of-pocket school fees and the related expenses. An average citizen who desires a university education has no choice but to swear his future into student loans, or he has to forever live with his high school diploma.

Worse still, economies favor big corporations over small businesses in advanced countries. More than ninety percent of new businesses in the United States close down before their third-year anniversary. Big corporations with deep pockets dominate both the financial and government sectors. They can afford to place a lobbyist on their payroll who will turn around to influence any legislative bill to their advantage—an opportunity that small businesses may never have.

> *Anyone who desires success can achieve it if he is ready to subject himself to learning the principles that are associated with success.*

Guess what the big corporations' argument is? "We pay big taxes!"

However, despite the unfair treatments that average citizens suffer in this world, hope remains for *"small people."* Anyone who desires success can achieve it if he is ready to subject himself to learning the principles that are associated with success.

Key Points

➢ Success is a universal term that is used to describe an achievement.

➢ Money is not equivalent to success. You may have all the wealth quantifiable as the sand on the beach, but you may not be successful.

➢ The definition of success is incomplete without the incorporation of a desired product or result, sustainability or added security and satisfaction.

➢ Not all that glitters is gold. Many people celebrate immature success or, even worse, failure, when they need to sit down and strategize their next move for total achievement.

➢ There are three stages of product development: inception, maturation, and completion.

➢ There are no blurred lines between stages or classes in success. Either you are successful, or you are not, but there is no sitting on the fence. There is also a sharp distinction between those who are perceived to be successful because of their amassed wealth and those who are the actual success-bearers. Whoever falls in the middle of these is not successful.

➤ In the real world, the achievement of success is not easy.

➤ The nature of the governance and system setups in all countries (third, second or first world) have created an expanding gap between the acclaimed elites and the poor. It, therefore, takes extra effort to change levels.

THE MYSTERY OF SUCCESS

Allowing only ordinary ability and opportunity, we may explain success mainly by one word and that word is WORK! WORK!! WORK!!! WORK!!!!

Frederick Douglass

Things may come to those who wait, but only the things left by those who hustle.

Abraham Lincoln

No one understands better than Frederick Douglass that success is never a result of luck or an accidental happening. Here is a man who rose from the lowliest of all levels or ranks that any man can find himself to become a household name in his time and long after his demise. Douglass was an American slave. He could not have risen through the ranks in the absence of his doggedness, dedication, determination, and passion. He knew very early in life that he had to fight for everything he needed. He had to learn the game of survival. He was taught the art of reading letters by the wife of his master, an act the husband frowned heavily upon and deemed inappropriate. Due to the disapproval coming from the master, the lessons were abruptly put to an early end.

Nevertheless, Frederick did not allow such a happening to forestall his bright future. He began to interact with the children of Whites. He would also sift through any piece of written material as if he were looking for nuggets in the smooth sand of the beach. Later, power changed hands for Douglass, and he was sold to a master, Edward Covey, who showed him nothing but cruelty. He was wicked to Douglass and would strike him regularly. This practice soon stopped when Frederick confronted him and put an end to the inhuman behavior.

As a man who understood that his destiny lay in his own hands, Frederick yet took another step and set himself on the path to success. He made a run for the escape route and freed himself from the field of slavery. He began his new life in Massachusetts. Frederick endured the grueling days of surviving and came out at the other side a champion. Soon, he rose to fame and was well-known as an orator, abolitionist, a newspaper publisher and an intelligent author. He became the President of the Freedman's Savings Bank, a Consul-General and a Minister-Resident to the Republic of Haiti, a Marshal of the District of Columbia, and a Consul d'Affaires for the Dominican Republic. He achieved these after the Civil War. His achievements did not end there. He was the first man of African-American descent to receive a vote for the Presidential nomination during the Republican Convention held in the year 1888. By the time he died, no one could refer to him any longer as a slave boy. He had become a man, a force to reckoned with in life. He lived and impacted several generations after him. In all regards, Frederick Douglass was a successful man.

Success does not come cheaply. In fact, the price is very high, and only those who are willing to pay it can get anything. If personified, success can be referred to as a guest that never visits anyone uninvited. Its characteristics are rare, as it restricts its business to people who are willing to live by its rules. Success is not friends with undisciplined people; it will not pay them attention even though they may desire it. Success will also camouflage itself to ward off its undisciplined admirers and make an escape before they realize that it ever came to say hello. Meanwhile, as success beats mediocre expectations, it grants excellent opportunity to its earnest admirers. It will stay within their grasp as long as they can keep to its rules.

Success leaves daydreamers with a dangling hope that they might have it someday; whereas, their chances of grasping it are almost impossible. Why? Success does not entertain fantasy; it does not condone a lack of discipline. Also, it hates the *Theory of Randomness,* because the process violates its rules. Therefore, a gambler is out of luck! Anyone who believes he or she has stumbled into success needs to watch out for the reversal of his or her status. It will only be a matter of time. Success happens by conscious effort put into endeavors in a step-wise manner. Sooner or later, the wheel of success will readjust to its usual standard and weed out the unqualified.

Indeed, success is not cheap but pricey. It makes its admirer undergo the process of time to squeeze out the virtues of hard work and dedication. Success will not hand him any reward until he can prove how meticulous he has become.

The pathway to success is rough and tough. However, it is pliable to folks who are determined to succeed.

A daydreamer should not expect to have success until he has taken the proper steps of goal implementation and hard work. It is expedient also to state that someone who chooses the path of normalcy may never have a significant breakthrough in his lifetime.

> *Anyone who believes he or she has stumbled into success needs to watch out for the reversal of his or her status. It will only be a matter of time.*

Since virtually every field is saturated by success admirers, the person must be willing to take the journey of an extra mile before he can succeed. He must have something new to display, and he must have an unusual approach to his practices before he can come out strong and excel.

Folks who dominate their field of operations are those who choose not to be complacent with the *slave-man mentality*: "I work more, you pay me less!" Success-minded people share a rare ideology to excel in whatever they do. They are critical thinkers with unusual views. They also behave like tigers that never oversleep. They are alert to their surrounding factors and are ready to grab an opportunity as soon as it crosses their path.

A success-minded person is not the same as an average Joe who lives a dry lifestyle. An average Joe will quickly accept a defeat and rationalize any failure to be his destiny. An average Joe cannot ply a success roadmap, because the stake will be too high for him. The word struggle is missing from his dictionary! An average Joe will instead prefer to stand by the roadside to criticize people that are making an effort. He can only whine about his uncomfortable situation, but he will not do anything out of the ordinary to deal with it. Meanwhile, a real success admirer hates the word *defeat*. He believes fate responds to an action, and he will do whatever life requires to improve his status.

A success-minded person is dangerous in his pursuit of success; he will fight any obstacle that comes his way. A typical success admirer will attempt to solve problems all night till daybreak. He will not rest until he has dealt a significant blow to a situation that wants to obstruct his progress.

How Fair Is Life?

"Life is not fair," said someone, but how true is this statement? If life is not fair, how come it only rewards people of certain characteristics and at the same time cuts off the majority of others? The statement "life is not fair" may sound good, but it lacks any justifiable backing. Life is fair, because it only positively rewards people who live by the principle of success. Honestly, life does not present everyone equal amounts of opportunity, but it does give everyone his or her chance to succeed. The choice is left to every individual to make a good use of his opportunity as it comes.

Opportunity often visits people randomly. It comes unannounced, and it might find its escape route sooner than imagined. Someone who is insensitive to his opportunity may lose it and end up spending the rest of his life waiting for it to return. A person must be sensitive and disciplined to discover an opportunity and make a good use of it. He must grab the opportunity and run with it as soon as it appears on his radar.

Two categories of people find it difficult to make good use of their opportunities. These are folks who celebrate false ideologies about life and those who have legitimate reasons to fail and have decided to tread that path. People who share wrongful ideologies believe they are destined to be poor, and they live up to that standard. They think that success is not meant for everyone; some people have to be poor for others to be rich. They believe they are the unfortunate set that must remain poor. Therefore, they live up to their belief. These people will not do anything out of the ordinary to influence their statuses. The irony of the situation is the fact that these hardliners also grumble about rich people. They hold everyone in their circle responsible for their poverty status. They typically blame their parents, bosses, and the government. What a life!

People who are victims of life's circumstances do themselves an injustice when they decide to accept their defeat! Their victim mentality worsens their situations since they became demoralized and are unable to rebound to a prospecting status. Unfortunately, life pities no one, and it will not earn these people success! Indeed, they might have been actual victims in the sense that they did not deserve what they suffered. However, life still will not care to give them success until they have put the past behind them and make meaningful progress! In other words, these people must stop the pity party, step away from their ashes, shake off their dust, and do something useful with their lives. It may be hard to hear, but it is true!

Admire Success Achievers

Someone who desires success will do him or herself a good deed by studying the lives of people who are already successful. The education he has can motivate him to ply a similar roadmap and become successful. Of course, the person does not need to be a copycat but can be inspired by their success stories. Meanwhile, not everyone in the success circle can be studied; only those who hailed from a humble background and displayed unique characteristics to break free to the success realm ought to be examined. The folks fit for this target study had every reason to accept their fate and live within the status quo, but they refused. Unlike many others who had personal dreams, they chose to act differently by refusing to pocket their goals. They thought of actualizing their ideas, and they made it happen.

Successful individuals that ought to be emulated are those that have both critical thinking and creative abilities. They can make the best of their dreams, they can detect a problem, and they can create a solution for it. These people can envisage an issue long before it comes up and can create a solution pathway for it. They sometimes also go beyond attempting to personally solve their problems by building a coalition or task force behind a challenge to ensure a formidable solution.

Admirable successful folks are curious individuals who are willing to find the cause of any subject matter for the betterment of lives and their success. These people don't easily give up on their convictions. They are ready to give whatever the situation will require and keep pushing their ideas until they spill out success.

Folks who follow the principles of success are not ditchers who work at will. They are dedicated individuals who diligently take care of their businesses. They don't take a break very often, but they are completely sold on to their aspiration and won't leave their work until they have made a significant dent in the problem. More importantly, these folks are not resource-wasters. They are disciplined to know how to manage their limited resources for higher output.

Life is full of success achievers: Some are no longer with us, and many are still contributing to successful endeavors. The list of individuals who followed the rules to become successful include Ben Franklin, Thomas Edison, Bill Gates, Warren Buffet, and Mark Zuckerberg.

Grab a seat and think!

Bill Gates had the conviction that the world needed a better method of handling their business activities than using large, mainframe computers. He was passionate about his conviction and wanted to make a difference. Therefore, he delved into researching how he could build software suitable enough to run on personal computers. Gates took his roadmap seriously. In an attempt to actualize his dream, he sometimes slept in the computer mainframe room as he tried different possibilities of realizing his dream. Gates' relentless effort eventually paid off, as he developed word-processing software that was fit for a personal computer. With improvement of his discovery, Gates copyrighted the widely accepted *Microsoft Office* that virtually everyone in the civilized world runs on his or her computer. Of course, Bill Gates became one of the wealthiest men on Earth afterward!

Warren Buffet did not invent the chain business idea, neither did Mark Zuckerberg create social media. However, these two individuals saw the opportunities that other people did not see (or saw but never attempted). Each of them saw the possibility of improving an existing service for progress. They stood to the particular challenge and pursued their visions.

Warren Buffet, in his ingenuity and dedication, refused to consider the practice of running a chain business as a mere source of income; he viewed it as an investment. He transmogrified his business into trade, and the effort spilled success for him! Mark Zuckerberg was also brilliant enough to derive inspiration from his college social network to pursue an idea of networking the whole world. Zuckerberg made a success of *Facebook*, which now daily serves billions of people on the planet. Individuals and businesses now take to *Facebook* on a daily basis for their operations. Must it still be mentioned that Warren Buffet and Mark Zuckerberg became significantly successful because they played by the rules of success?

A success-aspiring person must be able to detect an opportunity from a distance. He must have a plan to tap the break, and he must do something about it. This is more than merely stating the obvious; he must be dynamic at knowing how to put the pieces of opportunities together and make sense out of them.

It must be reinforced that folks who are insensitive to their opportunities and those who lack critical thinking abilities paired with hard work will find it difficult to forge ahead in life. A success-aspiring person must be able to detect an opportunity from a distance. He must have a plan to tap the break, and he must do something about it. This is more than merely stating the obvious; he must be dynamic at knowing how to put the pieces of opportunities together and make sense out of them. Why pieces? An opportunity rarely comes as a ready-made package. It comes in fragments, and it takes a person with deep insight to rearrange the pieces and make sense out of them.

Key Points

➤ You must be ready to pay the price of success if you ever have the desire to attain it. It is an expensive expenditure.

➤ Success does not crash parties. It must be invited before it comes. What you engage in most of the time is the determinant of whether you are chasing success away or extending an open hand to it.

➤ Daydreamers are only in pursuit of the idea of success but never the real deal.

➤ The Theories of Randomness and Success run on two parallel lines that can never meet.

➤ The slave-man mentality of "I work more, and you pay less" gets you nowhere with success.

➤ Life is very fair. You get the reward of whatever you introduce into its system. It is GIGO: Garbage In, Garbage Out.

➤ Opportunities do not come every day. Hence, when you see one, do not hesitate to make excellent use of it. Those who have made it never let the golden chances pass them by.

➤ There are two sets of people who find it extremely hard to latch on to opportunities presented to them. The first are those who have their minds filled with false ideologies and exalt them above every other thing. The second set includes those who made failure a choice.

➤ Just like every other thing, success has its rules that must be adhered to before the result can become evident. Those who have followed them are the ones who have the success stories to share.

SUCCESS CHARACTERISTICS

It is astonishing what an effort it seems to be for many people to put their brains definitely and systematically to work.

Thomas Edison

The house was not always tranquil. The norm was brawling and its accompanying cacophony. Of course, the father would often come home drunk in the dead of night. The mother would sometimes cower in the corner of the room, holding the child to her heart as if to ward off the drunken words coming from the man. The nights were usually the worst. He was always at work during the day. Those times were when he enjoyed himself.

You might be familiar with or at least imagine living or growing in that type of toxic environment. How do you like the picture generated? I am sure the answer is a resounding "Not at all," because no one wants to live in an atmosphere full of constant trouble. That is the picture of what Harry Reid's home looked while he was growing up.

Born in a mining town known as Searchlight in the heart of Nevada to a father who was a miner and an alcoholic, Reid had it rough. His father's highest educational level was elementary school. The mother, on the other hand, worked as a laundry lady. Her regular supply of work came from the brothels in the town. It was difficult to provide food for the family, and everyone made to do with anything that was provided. Reid learned early in life the art of surviving physical violence. He often used his fists to get his way. He was rough and tough. He took to boxing and would sometimes compete in locally organized competitions as an amateur. On other days, he would get involved in unexpected street rumbles.

Reid's success is an indication that anyone can change the course of their lives if they wish. Reid went on to graduate from Utah State University and proceeded to George Washington University's Law School. While he was studying, he got a night security job just to augment his family's income. After his graduation, he went on to practice his profession for a while before being elected in 1967 to the Nevada State Assembly. He then proceeded to serve as Lieutenant Governor. It was not all smooth and rosy for Reid. In 1974, he lost the senatorial election. He did not stop chasing his dream because of that. In 1982, he gave it another try and got elected as a US Senator. From then on, Reid continued to move steadily through the ranks with a little hitch once in a while.

Now and then, some individuals ask questions like "ARE SUCCESSFUL PEOPLE SUPER-HUMANS?"

Before I answer that question, consider another man, Thomas Edison. Oh! There is no more fabulous household name than that. He is the first inventor whose work we see every morning when we wake up: the first commercially acceptable incandescent lamp. Apart from the well-known story that he tried quite many different methods with many trials before he got it right, you probably did not know that this man got thrown out of school. Oh yes, he did. Edison was asked to be excused from the educational system because he got easily distracted in class. Then, his Supermom came to the rescue. Edison was home-schooled by his mother. Also, Edison got his first significant setback in life at a very young age. He lost nearly all his ability to hear. However, this almost-deaf, school drop-out went on to become the greatest inventor of all time. I believe you now have the answer to the question, but I will address it in the next few lines.

An individual once asked if successful people are super-humans. The answer is no! People who are successful are far from being extraordinary. They are ordinary people who choose not to follow the pathway of the majority in their pursuit of success. These people also have blood running in their veins like other regular human beings. They have twenty-four hours of the day as we do to run their activities, and many of them have loads of responsibilities on their shoulders as well.

Successful people face the same life challenges as everyone else. A few of them have serious problems, which sometimes relate to relationships, health, or finance. Some of these folks also have horrific pasts that may include abuse and not having basic needs met. Meanwhile, despite the odds, they were still able to sustain their hopes and dreams by refusing to let their circumstances keep them down. They kept resisting their uncomfortable situations until life turned to their favor.

Successful people live and breathe under the universal law of success like everyone else. Life sometimes presents them with limited resources as it does others. If someone questions these people's courage, he should not be surprised

> *Successful people face the same life challenges as everyone else.*

at the answer. They dared to violate the common-man cynicism of failure! They decided to operate by the guiding rule of success that folks in the mainstream would not care about or want to know.

A critical study of folks who are successful reveals they are ordinary individuals who focused on developing their abilities. They have their five senses trained to woo success, training that I will help you with in this book. They can recognize an opportunity from a distance, pursue it, and make a good use of it.

People have the choice to criticize those who are successful, but it would be better to applaud them for their courage. Instead of ranting against these people, folks who aspire to acquire success ought to move closer to learn their success secrets; maybe they can gain one or two ideas to their advantage.

Folks who are in the success circle are not necessarily dubious, as some might think. They are rare people that operate with different traits: They work with a reverse gear to cast the shadow of illusion on their spectators, perhaps to cover their tracks from their desperate critics.

> *People have the choice to criticize those who are successful, but it would be better to applaud them for their courage.*

Consider this: Rich people pay Uncle Sam their fair share of taxes after they have counted their losses. The majority of others pay more than thirty-five percent of their earnings upfront to IRS, even before calculating their losses. Who is wiser?

Success-conscious people don't travel in the same traffic with everyday people. They do not follow the crowd; often choosing to have a head-on collision with challenges as other people run away.

Successful folks are informed and alert to their surroundings. They have sharp minds and eagle eyes. They are skilled at tasking their minds for creativity and ingenuity. They don't go with the flow of traffic. They aren't naïve to entertain the cooked-up stories that often fly around; they are personally out there, uncovering dirt to discover first-hand resources that can benefit them.

Folks that operate in the success circle have an in-depth knowledge of their career, but they often don't show it. They will instead declare themselves as good students who desire to know more. They are eager to learn to improve their skills. They can stay up all night reading, researching, and brainstorming to initiate and perfect a plan that can improve their status. These folks have the resilient ability to take up any challenge that would quickly cripple others. They are unafraid of an obstacle. They will confront it with persistence until the impediment fizzles out.

Success-conscious people don't travel in the same traffic with everyday people. They do not follow the crowd; often choosing to have a head-on collision with challenges as other people run away.

Folks in the success circle surf against tides with a calculated mind. They are strategic planners, and they mostly stay ahead of any game that associates with their exploits. They have plans to guide them. At the same time, they are flexible, because they have launch-ready backup plans should their forecast fail. They will put them into action without losing ground to their competitors.

Successful folks have made their mistakes and learned from them. They know how to navigate around low odds, and they also know how to generate real results. They are professionals. They don't scratch a thing on the surface and claim to have its full knowledge. They are prudent people who delve into the root of a matter to understand what it's all about. In short, they don't stop in pursuing their exploit until they have made a successful product of it.

Successful folks act outside of the routine to achieve their goals. They are indifferent to the redundant human cycle of sleep, wake, eat, work, make money, spend money, sleep, and wake. They stay focused to crack the code of success. These are fighters who don't take a "no" for an answer. They will give whatever life demands to have their expectations met. These smart people are not afraid of their problems; they viciously attack them at a fast rate. They don't allow a challenge to sit around for too long before they attempt to solve it. They also don't believe there exists any problem that is unsolvable. They will work all day and all night to troubleshoot a problem until they can find a solution for it, or at least alleviate the impact of the problem. No wonder they can crack the secret code of success!

Don't hate folks who are successful. Emulate their tenacity.

People who are successful are not only elite in wealth; they are also elite in value. They are people who make excellent choices. They have an unusual approach to addressing their ordeals. They prefer to label it "a challenge" than to call it "a problem." These folks see a half-full cup; they don't see a half-empty cup. Not only do they have a positive outlook, but they also dare to take a proactive step into filling their half-full cup to its brim.

Quality reigns in the domain of successful people. They have a taste for quality! They don't settle for shrubs but go for trees! They will give whatever it takes to map out a strategy that can make their product yield lasting success.

Is Success Achievable?

As a man thinks in his heart, so is he!

King Solomon

We do not always share similar opportunities, but everyone is bound by the universal law of success and can be successful. That is, one can still achieve success whether he was born to an affluent family or not. Everyone has at least one facet of potential that can help him or her become successful. Unfortunately, many people focus all their attention on money, as if it's the only tool needed to generate success. As I have mentioned, money plays an important role, but it's not enough to create success. In fact, someone who has money today may become poor in the near future if he lacks other essential elements of success.

Besides finances, a person must adequately shape his mindset to befit the success that he hopes for. His mind must be in the proper place for the expected success to become his. The person must have personal confidence that he has what it takes to become successful.

> *Everyone has at least one facet of potential that can help him or her become successful.*

Whether he comes from an affluent family or not, he must be able to tell himself, "My future is bright, and I can become successful!" Meanwhile, for this assertion to yield a positive result, he must be willing to pinpoint his areas of strength and weakness and work on both. He should improve his areas of strength to grow his prospects, while at the same time bringing gradual improvement to his weak points for an added advantage on his success roadmap.

A tree does not make a forest; someone who has discovered his abilities may soon realize that he needs some helping hands to achieve his goals. He must not hesitate to seek that help. Once all plans are in place, the person must engage his work with full determination. He will face some challenges as he embarks on his success roadmap, but he can't stop, neither can he slow down. He must push through his challenges to achieve his success expectations.

Key Points

➤ All humans are made equally and are subject to same universal law of success. Everyone can succeed without the success of a person negatively affecting the other.

➤ Success loves and hates everyone equally. It will only favor those who live by its rules.

➤ The rich are humans; they face similar challenges as others, but they react differently.

➤ The rich are not fools; they are clever to turn their odds around to their advantage.

➤ Lack of finances may not be the major player in a man's failure. His mindset may be his worst enemy.

➤ A success-minded person understands the rules that pertain to success. He is ready to offer the sacrifice that success requires. He will fight for surviving. He will buy knowledge; he will build a success skill-set and fine tune it.

➤ A man of success will navigate around his limitations. He will make a detour to intercept success. Once having grabbed the bull by its horns, he will make the best of it.

➤ Not all success admirers have the guts to make it. Those unwilling or unable to go the distance are filtered out of the race to success.

➤ Success is canny and in warding off indecisive aspirants.

➤ Mr. Success is not so stupid as to follow purposeless people.

➤ Folks in the success circle eschew common-man traditions of accepting failure as fate.

➤ A few successes might come easily, but many will surface with some challenges to overcome.

➤ The roadmap toward achieving success may be tough, but the reward is priceless. Slowly but surely, hard work will pay off for a dedicated person.

➤ A statement such as "someone's independent ability to stir his mind to pursue and achieve success" ought to be included in any definition given to a complete man. Such an assertion will help him to understand his need to explore his opportunities and make the best of them.

HUMAN FAILURE FACTORS

In reading the lives of great men, I found that the first victory they won was over themselves…

Harry S. Truman

Humans have potential for success but, at the same time, humans are confronted with plagues that inhibit their success potential. The inhibiting factors are: procrastination, indulgence, obstinacy, complacency, poor judgment, and fear. These factors first slow down any effort to attain success and eventually block the success path when an appropriate action is not taken within a reasonable time.

Procrastination

Procrastination is the thief of success.

James Taiwo

Procrastination is the *"thief of time."* It is also the *"thief of success."* Massive opportunities are lost on a daily basis due to procrastination! The epidemic is rampant in society as people find it more convenient to enjoy their state of complacency than moving forward. This attitude is encouraged with the advent of technology. However, while most people have lost control to this plague, a few individuals are still disciplined enough to escape it. They have the same reasons to procrastinate, but they choose not to follow that path.

The habit of procrastination does not follow the principles of success at all. It is an impossible deviant! Whether or not the reason to adopt the practice is justifiable, someone who procrastinates needs to face the fact that his or her work will not have any meaningful progress until the method is corrected.

Everyone that procrastinates will always have a reason for his action. A typical procrastinator will often give excuses in the manner of the following statements:

- "I will do it later. Why the rush?"

- "I have something more important to do right now."

- "I need some rest to have more energy for this."

- "Why the stress now when I have plenty of time later?"

- "If I do this later, the result may not be that bad."

- "If I do it now, I won't find something else to do later."

- "Ain't going nowhere. I have plenty of time."

The common denominators of all the excuses listed above are "false hope!" The statements sound un-harmful, and any procrastinator can escape using them. Meanwhile, no matter how reasonable the comments seem, they all lead to zero results!

Whether or not the reason to adopt the practice is justifiable, someone who procrastinates needs to face the fact that his or her work will not have any meaningful progress until the method is corrected.

Indulgence

Indulgence is the worse disease of all time!

James Taiwo

Indulgence is a subtle factor of failure that hinders a person from fully manifesting his potential. The trait is similar to procrastination, but a bit different. Unlike a procrastinator who may not know what he misses, an indulgent person knows what benefit is at stake, but he is just not making use of the advantage.

Indulgent people usually hedge around an issue when they ought to tackle it for a possible solution. Even when they know what to do, they will still choose to hold back. They rarely take any initiative to improve their success morale. Folks in the indulgent category have poor work ethics. They rarely stand up to their responsibility. A person with the typical indulgent attitude will prefer to say, "It's their job, not mine!"

The root of indulgence is traceable to secret fear. Such an individual is afraid of the consequences of his actions. He fears what will happen to him if he takes drastic steps with benefits embedded in them. Based on any given situation, an indulgent person may think of financial burden. A person

> *The root of indulgence is traceable to secret fear.*

who suffers from indulgence must take a practical approach to addressing his situation. He needs to be courageous and take a measurable risk. To break free, he must allow the reality of a situation to prove itself. Whether he passes or fails, his reasonable attempt will set him free, and he will begin to make necessary success progress.

Obstinacy

Obstinacy - a defiant destroyer of the success roadmap!

James Taiwo

Obstinacy is an alternate word used for stubbornness. Nothing is fanciful about this trait, which tends to crush anyone's success exploits. Obstinacy is "determination used negatively." Obstinacy blindfolds and traps its victims to only pay attention to personal feeling and self-worth, while they are blinded from seeing the beneficial external influences. Victims of stubbornness are locked in one-way traffic. They operate with a closed mind and are not open to outside contributions. A decision must go their way, or nothing else happens. Obstinate people do not entertain dialog; they don't like negotiation nor do they consider other people's views. Whatever they say is final.

Have you met an obstinate person, or maybe you are one? An obstinate person is not different from a careless driver with tunnel vision, who prefers only to pay attention to his favorite road signs but shuns other cautionary warnings that might save his life. It takes an unfortunate incident to happen before an obstinate person would consider revising his viewpoint. No pain, no reasoning!

People with obstinate characteristics have equal chances of success and failure. They have strong determination, but they lack common sense. If you see these folks successful today, be expecting to see them declaring bankruptcy tomorrow. Obstinate people applaud themselves for their strong determination. However, the same characteristic can turn to become their failure factor, because they are unresponsive to possible evolving factors that influence their work.

Obstinacy cannot be overlooked on the success road trip. A person who aspires to success must not allow this plague to ruin him. Something good about stubbornness is the fact that it is a dominant trait that can easily be detected. A person

> *Victims of stubbornness are locked in one-way traffic. They operate with a closed mind and are not open to outside contributions.*

can find out quickly if he suffers from it. A quick means of identification is to question oneself.

It will be helpful to ask yourself some of the following questions to know if you are a victim of obstinacy. What you also need to know is that you must to answer them honestly for you to see the truth about yourself.

➤ Do I take an offense when other people oppose my idea?

➤ Do I take time to reflect on other people's opinions?

➤ Do I venture for more knowledge in my field of operation?

➤ Do I have anyone in my life that I can consider as a mentor?

If you answered "yes" to one or more, it may be helpful for you to fall in love with the word "submission," as in your submission to the fact that you are not an all-knowing human being. This is a pathway to getting the solution to the problem of obstinacy. Be submissive enough to accept the fact that you are not a perfect person; you are subject to failure like every other person. You are not self-sufficient: your education and experience alone are not enough to earn you success, neither are they adequate to sustain you. Contributions from other sources can aid your success.

A decision to disengage from obstinacy will allow an influx of fresh ideas that can help you maintain a smooth and prospective exercise that leads to sound achievement.

Your submission to the fact that you are not an all-knowing human being. This is a pathway to getting the solution to the problem of obstinacy.

Complacency

*Success breeds complacency. Complacency breeds
failure. Only the paranoid survive.*

Andy Grove

*You need to have a redesign because familiarity
breeds a kind of complacency.*

Timothy White

Complacent people are folks who are trapped in their typical routine. They care less about the outcome of their efforts and more about achieving a comfortable state of mind. These folks don't do anything out of the ordinary; they are unwilling to go the extra mile for their possible growth.

Folks who are complacent with their status are hypersensitive to and repulsed by to any factor that may tend to influence it. Those who are complacent have restricted mindsets that will only allow them to stick with their customary practices, which may have lost relevance. Complacent people will defend their positions with a Stone Age philosophy but care less about how new technology is influencing their fields of operation. Their nonchalant attitude causes them to lose their competitive edge over others who are flexible enough to adapt to the new developments.

> *Those who are complacent have restricted mindsets that will only allow them to stick with their customary practices, which may have lost relevance.*

Complacency is not hard to build. A person who enjoys his status and avoids challenges will enter into a state of complacency. The mind will experience the benefit it finds, and if left uninterrupted, the process will degenerate into a routine. The mind will derive satisfaction in it and repel any other activity that may intend to influence it. This is complacency!

A person can be free from the state of complacency if he is ready to task his mind beyond what it entertains. The breaking-free process requires that a person who is affected takes a practical step that will expose him to new learning, which can be outsourced to the school system and public library. He must read useful books that can reorient his mind into proper thought processing. However, irrespective of the learning method adopted, a person who intends to break free from the state of complacency must engage in a practical exercise that will influence the mind to behave beyond its comfortable norm.

Poor Judgment

*The wise builds on the rock, but the foolish builds
in sand.*

Jesus Christ

Most of the failures that humans encounter are attributable to poor decisions. Poor decision making creates a huge impact on health, family, finances, education, career, and a host of other factors. Most importantly, humans make poor decisions of their time usage. A typical human will spend significant time on activities that are far from achieving useful contributions to their successful growth. A few poor decisions that humans make are listed below.

➢ Humans yield limitless attention for recreation but allow limited attention span for any prospective training. An average human offers thirty minutes of attention in class while they show different attitudes in the movie theatre.

➢ Humans can stay up all night to watch their favorite show at the expense of the necessary rest their bodies need to recuperate.

➢ Humans buy branded items; they acquire the latest mobile gadgets, but they default on their bill payments.

➢ Humans liberally cheap-chat on their computing devices; they play video games and watch insensate videos. However, they don't bother to use the same tools for research that can add intrinsic value to their lives.

➢ Typical humans are comfortable consumers; they don't aspire

51

to produce anything valuable for others. An average human believes, "They give it, I use it!"

No one is excused from the category of people who make poor decisions. People of various statuses—the educated and the illiterate, the rich and the poor—have made poor decisions. They make poor choices that are detrimental to successful growth. Meanwhile, not all people consistently make poor decisions. Some folks learn quickly from their mistakes and make corrections. Some others partake in

> *No one is excused from the category of people who make poor decisions.*

poor decision-making by turning it into their regular practice. Those are the people who stand by as spectators while others are advancing on their success road trip.

Humans are not perfect, and no one is able to make the right decision at all times. However, while sporadic, inadequate decisions can be overlooked, a numerous count will result in disaster! A problem will arise if the gravity of any poor choice outweighs other remaining factors.

Irrespective of the count, some decisions create more impact than others. A decision difficult enough to wreck a venture should be carefully considered before it is made. The exploit may survive the little infractions of minor poor decisions but not pronounced ones. For example, a person who drives five miles to save five cents on gasoline prices is making a poor judgment call, but this is easily forgiven. However, a person who invested his hard-earned money in the stock market without proper knowledge of how it works has made a significant poor decision that may wreck him for life. A person who hired-to-purchase a new car from the dealer without having the income to pay his monthly note may successfully impress his friends today, but he will soon walk barefooted and seek help from the same friends.

A person can improve on the practice of making erratic decisions by reducing the speed of his decision-making process. To avoid making a costly mistake, he must give himself ample time to process his thoughts, carefully consider his options and decide if his decision is beneficial. Under careful evaluation, he may realize some ideas he earlier considered as prospective are merely useless. Had he implemented them they would have affected his efforts.

In addition to personal evaluation of a decision, a person should also consult people who are already skilled in the field of interest to gather some knowledge. Experienced folks have a history of successes and failures. They can envision if an idea is prospective or not. Their contributions may create a significant positive impact during the process of decision evaluation.

> *A person can improve on the practice of making erratic decisions by reducing the speed of his decision-making process.*

In summary, a success-aspiring person should consider these three essential factors:

> ➤ Don't start an initiative that you are not fully prepared to pursue.

> ➤ Don't implement a change that you are not ready to follow through on.

> ➤ Don't launch a new venture if you are aware of imminent interruption.

Fear Factor

*Fear creates a fake impression that establishes a
real limitation.*

James Taiwo

You must have heard of the Wright brothers—the inventors of
the first commercially viable aircraft. Well, while these gentlemen
were credited because they turned the course of aeronautics around
for good with their invention, it is also widely known that they were
not the first set of people to ever fly an aircraft. Many people,
including Gustav Whitehead, Alphonse Penaud, Octave Chanute,
tried before them. They all, in one way or another, set the ground on
which the Wright brothers built theirs.

The point of interest here is not the Wright brothers, but one of
the earlier inventors, Alphonse Penaud, who was a French aeronautic
engineer. He is credited with being the first person to employ the use
of twisted rubber bands as a generator of motive power in the
designing of a helicopter. This method is still widely used today in
the making of airplane toys for children.

In 1876, Penaud made the first commercially stable airplane with
a design very similar to what we use today. He called it the
Planophore. His version of the aircraft came with a joystick that
could be utilized in the control of the rudders, both vertical and
horizontal. This idea was also significantly improved upon by the
Wright brothers, although Penaud gave them the template.

Unfortunately, despite the achievement that could have gone
ahead to improve lives back then, Penaud ended his life prematurely

at the age of thirty. What was the reason for this action? He gave in to one of the failure factors that are inherent in everyone and would rear their ugly heads if allowed. Penaud could not obtain the financial assistance that he needed to fund his project. Therefore, fear got the ground and gave rise to depression. Under this heavy influence, Penaud ended his own life.

Every human has a tendency to nurse fear in his mind. It comes with a reflex action, and it is naturally displayed by everyone. Fear has a biological background that is traceable to the human hormone adrenaline, also known as the fight or flight hormone. The hormone causes a person to agitate when an unprecedented circumstance arises.

Fear by itself is not evil. It can be a motivational source of challenge to persuade anyone into making a positive effort. For example, a person who is afraid of what his future holds can be challenged to start taking some beneficial steps toward changing it. Also, fear of the future can force a wasteful person to start saving money if he is unsure of what next may happen to him.

Despite the few opportunities that fear can bring its host, it is still considered an enemy of success. Fear does more harm than good! In most cases, it hunts its hosts and forces them to focus their minds on an imaginary ghost in their pursuit. Fear creates a false impression and manipulates people into acting contrarily to the reality of what is happening around them.

Fear may camouflage itself in many colors. Its victims do not know how they ended up being trapped. They are sunk into the mire and don't understand the cause. Unfortunately, fear never tells anyone "I am coming to take control of your life!" Fear does not operate in isolation; anxiety often accompanies it. These friends, fear and anxiety, work hand-in-hand to create their havoc.

Anxiety causes its host to care about irrelevant matters. A victim of anxiety will worry about a question that someone may never ask him in his lifetime. Prisoners of anxiety are bound by difficult questions: "What if, what then, what after, what next?" An anxious person becomes fearful when he can't find an answer to his question.

> *Fear does not operate in isolation; anxiety often accompanies it.*

Fear plays its dirty tricks on an agitated person and causes him to react to any given situation inappropriately. Fear can damage a person's nervous system; it can cause high blood pressure. Fear can even kill a person! Anyone who is significantly afraid of any one thing should consult his doctor, visit a therapist, and pray to God.

Fear hinders a person from putting his full abilities to use. It can cause a person to become overly sensitive and divert his attention from issues that are important. Fear drains energy. It can hinder a person from making taking the initiative. A fearful person has a fragile mind, which is disadvantageous to the success roadmap. A typical timid person will not attempt new things because he doesn't want to fail.

A person who intends to break free from fear must question himself on some personal matters and provide candid answers to the following questions:

➢ Why should I be afraid about this matter?

➢ What am I really afraid of?

➢ What is the worst that can happen if I face my fear?

➢ Do I have anything within my power to overcome this

situation that gives me cold feet?

A person who discovers that he or she has the power to conquer his fear should not hesitate to take action. If he can't overcome the situation, he should stop wasting his mind and time on it. Instead, he should be proactive to consult people who are trained to handle the situation.

> *A person who discovers that he or she has the power to conquer his fear should not hesitate to take action.*

A success-aspiring person cannot afford to operate in fear! He must take the necessary steps to improve his situation. Once the proper steps have been taken, he should stop being overly concerned and allow the case to play out by itself. The break in his thought pattern will help him to have a clear understanding of the situation for education and improvement.

Key Points

➤ Procrastination is not only the thief of time but of success, destiny, and resources.

➤ Many people have been lost to oblivion because they could not rouse themselves to do whatever was needed at the right time.

➤ Procrastination feeds on false hope, and the more it gets fed, the stronger it becomes. Subsequently, the harder it becomes to break free.

- The antidote to procrastination is discipline.
- If you prefer to push jobs to others knowing wholly or partially what is at stake, you are indulgent.
- If you have the desire to go fast, you could walk alone, but if you ever wish to go far in life, walk with a team.
- Obstinacy will prevent you from seeing what is useful in what others are saying or doing.
- A stubborn person often has the desired trait of determination, but he couples it with a lack of common sense. He may end up going nowhere near success.
- The opposite of obstinacy is submission. The more you exhibit it, the higher you get lifted.
- Complacency creeps in almost undetected. You should actively engage your mind and challenge the status quo to eradicate it.
- Poor judgment can cripple you if it is allowed.
- Carry out your due diligence before taking crucial steps.
- Not every act of poor judgment is forgivable.
- Not every poor person lacks judgment. Choose to act wisely at all times.
- Let fear serve you. Turn it to a motivating factor.
- Let fear push your inquisitive button for research and education.
- Let fear push you into making proactive decisions for a positive future.

> ➤ Question fearful elements to lessen their stings.

> ➤ Fear has no base, but it accumulates strength over time.

> ➤ The more inappropriate attention fear receives, the more muscle it builds.

THE ESSENTIAL FACTORS OF SUCCESS

I'm more afraid of success than failure. Success makes us so sure of ourselves that we do not analyze the factors that lead us to our success.

Jorge Valdano

Resources

A person needs resources to drive his or her goals. He needs time, energy, and funding. He also needs moral support. These resources are essential to achieving success. Their absence will make any effort toward success suffer a major setback and cause bumps in the success roadmap.

The resources that are needed to achieving success are not equally shared among all people. Some people have more than others. This applies especially to finances as a resource. Funding favors some above others based on those that surround them (in terms of family and friends). Folks who are born to the affluent family can quickly tap into some family reserve. A person who has a poor background may not have a similar benefit. Such a person would

No less-privileged person should underrate himself on the success pathway.

have to struggle to get a financial backup for his plans. However, no less-privileged person should underrate himself on the success pathway. His life is worth as much as others'; he has his chance of achieving success.

No one has a justifiable excuse for failure; everyone must venture to succeed at all costs! The person who suffers from inadequate resources should not fold; he should attempt to get his needed resources from the available sources. Sometimes, he may have to juggle between different ventures and test various grounds to mine his opportunity. Overall, the end goal will reward his relentless efforts.

On the other side of the tracks, those born into affluence need to realize that finances are not all you need for success. Adequate resources do not automatically transform into success-generation; a person in need of success must know how to make good use of resources before they can lead to success. That is, the resources necessary for success—funding, time, energy, and moral support— must be properly utilized and carefully combined to achieve any needed goal.

> *No one has a justifiable excuse for failure; everyone must venture to succeed at all costs!*

Funding

Almost no dream can materialize without funds. Many great dreams have died without funding, and this same issue has led many to an early grave. Question yourself on the issue of funds before you start to advertise your dream. Ask yourself, "Do I have enough funds to implement this dream?" If the answer is negative, further question yourself: "Where can I get the funds to implement this exercise?"

The worst thing a success-aspiring person can do is to fold his or her arms in hopes for some magic to happen. He must take a significant step to get his needed funds. He has an option to suspend the implementation of his dream and start to saving money that will support it. He also has a choice to borrow money and begin implementation immediately. You need to drop every element of pride for this to happen.

> *The worst thing a success-aspiring person can do is to fold his or her arms in hopes for some magic to happen.*

As a success-conscious person, you cannot be too arrogant to seek financial help from formidable sources. This includes family and friends. The first set of people to believe in you will likely come from this group. Draw up a financial plan and target to receive local financial support from friends. Explore the benefits of financial institutions. Walk into your local bank and share your vision with their manager. Promote your ideas with the use of prospective terms when consulting financial institutions. In spite of your big dreams, you need to sound very convincing. Promise them the incentive of your massive investment to their organization once your idea becomes successful. Throw in a lot of confidence here. Make up a sound business plan. If they are reluctant to take the risk of loaning you money, you need to give them reasons to change their minds. They work with facts and results, not mere promises. You have to find a way to persuade them to contribute to your pilot program. Pitch a plan and show them the facts. Be confident in your speech and let a strong driving force be obvious.

Local banks are supportive. Many people don't realize that local banks offer great support for their neighbors. Local banks, such as community banks and cooperatives, are always on the lookout to support prospective local businesses. This gives you an edge over their distant clients. Banks will tend to support your local business on the claim that they are "helping" and offering a "payback" to the community. Of course, you know the deal; their target is to boost their reputation and make money. Meanwhile, you (their loan recipient) also win the game by having the financial resources you need to drive your goal. In the end, it's a win-win situation.

If it works or it doesn't work, do not stop your fund-sourcing at that. There are other ways to go about finding funding. Besides exploring the support of financial institutions, explore creative personal fundraising exercises. Also, some internet platforms offer fundraising support. Consider raising funds on social media. Some corporate websites also provide fundraising assistance. Sites such as GoFundMe, Kickstarter, and PayPal fall into this category. You may be surprised by how many people are out there who are willing to support the kind of work you intend to do.

Time

Another important resource is time. Time is an essential tool for success. It is a highly prized resource. In fact, the adage "time is money" is widely used everywhere around the world. Time is indeed a luxury and must be appropriately managed to achieve success. Anyone who wants success must know how to make good use of his time. If you can put every hour of the 24 hours you get in the 365 days in a year to proper use, you would have few or no regrets on looking back.

People who are disciplined with their time usage have an advantage over those who are not. They understand the principles of time management. Disciplined people separate their work hours from pleasure hours. They know when they should focus squarely on work. They don't engage in any activity that can distract them from doing their job. These folks are not engulfed by telephone conversations when they are working. They only take essential calls! They also don't socialize during work hours; they would rather switch off their phone or turn off their social apps on their mobile devices. These folks mean business, and they are on their way to having their dreams come true.

Folks who are disciplined allot time for their jobs. They estimate the possible time it will take to complete a task; they are determined to stick with the schedule. They don't pay attention to unnecessary

> *Time is an essential tool for success.*

feelings when they should be working. They understand that sticking to their schedule helps them to reach their goals. This practice ends up helping them to maintain focus and keep the momentum that will ultimately lead to their success.

As a success-conscious person, you must understand the value of your time and tap into it. *Make hay when the sun shines*; spend your time on valuable activities and avoid wasting time on irrelevant others. Be disciplined enough to invest your time in activities that have prospects and will generate

> *Be disciplined to not follow the crowd.*

tangible results! Be disciplined to not follow the crowd. Evaluate your actions and choose to focus on those you believe can help make your aspirations realized. Eliminate every activity that does not produce tangible results.

Energy

Human energy is needed to drive an aspiration to achieve physical benefits. Even the advanced technology that brings a new alternative source of energy is not adequate for success generation. The human brain has no substitute! At least no robot has the capability of supervising itself without causing problems. No other energy perfectly replaces that which is generated from the human body.

A success-aspiring person must understand that his mind is the brainpower of success. Understanding it is not enough; he must utilize it. He must exercise his intellectual ability to achieve his motive. Unfortunately, some folks don't understand the value of their human capacity. They stay idle and allow the benefit to go to waste! The energy wasters may have justifications for their idleness, but will those excuses earn them any tangible success? Laziness offers zero reward, irrespective of any excuses that a person provides.

Youths and young adults tend to misuse energy. They are aware of their fresh minds and physical strength, but they are also carried away by their power. Therefore, they tend to pursue pointless adventures just for the fun of it. Young people care less about the

The human brain has no substitute!

results of their ventures; they just want to prove what they are capable of achieving. These are wasters who, with the right perspective, can amount to great success. They have bright futures if they can channel their energy into proper courses. Some want to channel their energy, but fear is a major crippling factor.

66

Some people are afraid of failure, so they do not put their energy to use at all. They have aspirations and power but, unfortunately, they are not willing to take a leap. Meanwhile, nothing is wrong with a few trial-and-error steps that can lead to a success opportunity. A person has to take some risks to have a clear understanding of the type of

Youths and young adults tend to misuse energy. They are aware of their fresh minds and physical strength, but they are also carried away by their power.

success that is at stake. Of course, he must be careful not to experiment with a sensitive part of a goal, but he still needs to test the ground and explore any new opportunity that may unfold. During his diligent search, he will lay hands on a goal he is not willing to let go of. Having a goal is essential for success.

For a person to make a good use of his energy, he must have a particular goal in mind. Also, since he cannot operate blindly, he must comprehend his work to know how to act on it effectively. He mustn't direct his energy aimlessly. To achieve this, the person must task his mind to answer the question "Why?" If a supervisor assigns a task, he should be bold to question "why" and "how." The knowledge obtained will guide him throughout the implementation stage. He wouldn't work as someone put to forced labor. He can come up with suggestions and find a better alternative to get the job done efficiently.

Moral Support

The term *moral support* refers to outside support that a person receives that creates a positive psychological impact on him or her. An absence of moral backing creates negative mental implications. The help received cannot be physically quantified, but it leaves a significant imprint on the mind. Not everyone understands the impact that moral support creates. Therefore, some folks do not care to offer it when they should, or to take advantage of it when it is offered. Also, some people who are fortunate enough to receive moral support do not appreciate it. It seems worthless to them because, at that particular moment, the worth can't be converted into money.

Moral support sounds like a simple concept, but it carries significant weight and creates a substantial impact on the success roadmap. People who have it will have their agility aroused to pursue their dreams and have the opportunity to become successful. In contrast, folks who feel let down by their

> *Moral support sounds like a simple concept, but it carries significant weight and creates a substantial impact on the success roadmap.*

trusted friends and family members tend to lose their work enthusiasm. If one receives no moral support from those close to him, one's drive would be largely affected.

A person who feels he has lost enthusiasm for his work should question himself on the subject of moral support. If he determines his morale has dwindled as a result of a lack of moral support, he should not hesitate to seek a solution to the problem. More likely than not, his suffering may have something to do with the lack of support he receives from his loved ones. He may also be working in a hostile environment. However, there is a solution for this situation.

The solution for a lack of moral support may sound a bit harsh, but it is not unrealistic. The first solution must be to place high importance on his life. He must have self-confidence! He cannot achieve much success if he lacks self-esteem, even if he has the support of the whole world. The second solution is for a person who suffers from lack of moral support to distance himself from his indifferent or even hostile environment. He has to be accepted and appreciated for his mind to operate at a premium level. Therefore, he must put himself in a friendly atmosphere. The process of creating a positive environment may involve replacing some existing friends with new ones, or lessening his contact with his family. He may have to change his job group or leave an entire establishment if his work environment is volatile. It might not be easy to leave the familiar, but he must work around it to achieve the success he desires.

Ultimately, as a success-aspiring person, you must be sure not to drop your aspirations for the sake of dispelling the hostility or indifference from those you care about. Aim to have a stable relationship with some individuals who express belief in your dream and are ready to support it. Spend less time with the individuals (whether relatives or not) who demoralize you with their behavior. Why waste time with people whose attitudes obstruct your success pathway? The reality of life is that you don't need moral support

> *As a success-aspiring person, you must be sure not to drop your aspirations for the sake of dispelling the hostility or indifference from those you care about.*

from a particular set of people; anyone can meet the need. Sometimes a loved one may not share your dream, but that is not the end of the world. God always provides helping hands through someone, somewhere. The individual, if discovered, becomes your loved one—your guardian angel, whom you must celebrate when the rubber meets the road and your goal is achieved.

Remember that this is not restricted to those you've shown love to previously. It could be anyone. Therefore, be receptive to good people. You will recognize them when they come.

Key Points

➤ There are some factors that, when available, make the journey to success more leisurely. These include resources, funding, time, energy, and moral support.

➤ Anything (expendable or otherwise) that goes into the accomplishment of a project is a resource. Thus, this term encompasses the rest of the factors.

➤ Resources are limited while our wants are limitless.

➤ Resources are not equally shared among all of us. We are not born equal. While some are born with a silver spoon, some were born with a base metal spoon metallic while others came with the wooden type.

➤ How we get our resources, manage them, and use them is

dependent on us.

> Do not be too shy to approach others for assistance.

> Your time is money; you should spend it well. Whatever returns you get depend on what you invest most of your time on.

> Every person, especially youths, have a core of energy that should be directed to positive use.

> Surround yourself with people of like mind that can support you when you are losing your enthusiasm.

> In the same way you choose your friends, select the people in your career development. Mingle with people that you share core values with and who will propel you upward when things are taking a nosedive.

SUCCESS ROAD RAGE

A constant struggle, a ceaseless battle to bring success from inhospitable surroundings, is the price of all great achievements.

Orison Swett Marden

The beauty of any success road trip is to have smooth progress. However, it is unfortunate that some inhibiting factors often come up to negatively influence the journey. These "road rage" factors are tagged as *personal battles* and *external pressure*. They force the wheel of any adventure to drag. If any of the road rage factors is significant enough, it can completely stop a successful venture. Every success-conscious person must care enough to investigate how the road rage factors are influencing his work; he or she must also make a sizable effort to subdue the factors.

Personal Battles

We have established the fact that successful people are just like every other person. They have their ups and downs. They have those times, just like you and me, that they want to go out and be free, but it is nearly impossible for them, because they are always in the public eye. They also have times they would prefer to be alone, but the paparazzi will not let them be. They have their share of financial instability (remember, though, that success is not all about money), health problems, and family crises. Often, they have no one to share their hurt with because of their position in the society. Below are some of the struggles that people who have positively influenced humanity passed through in their lives.

Fame came to Neil Armstrong because of a particular event in his adult life. It is possible that he may have made other discoveries, but none was as significant as his near-miraculous trip to outer space; notably his journey to and walking on the moon. For years, many people, including me, had the notion that Neil Armstrong was the only one that completed that feat. However, he was not the only person on the jolly ride to the moon. In fact, there were three men: Neil Armstrong, Buzz Aldrin, and Michael Collins. However, Neil Armstrong was the captain of the spaceship, the crew, and the adventure. For approximately ninety minutes, the men poked at the moon and came back with exciting news for the inhabitants of planet Earth. Whatever they brought back with them would be utilized by several generations after them.

Reports have it that although the men had made a great accomplishment, their relationships with each other were far from savory. Although the three men did something that had never been done before by the human race, they could not salvage their friendships, especially because none had existed before the breakthrough on the moon. They overcame the law of gravity, but one person at least, among them, had to pay a great price for it. He talks openly about it. This individual was Buzz Aldrin, the second in command of the space flight and who, under normal circumstances, could have been the person to step first on the moon.

The first price he paid came through his mother. The woman, who felt that the apparent success that was somewhat inevitable for her son, took her life before it ever began. She foresaw the strains that it would impose on her son and left before it happened. It was a blow below the belt that rocked Buzz's life, coupled with the fact that there was no love lost between him and his boss. While Buzz does not talk much about whatever went down that day on the moon, he sure has no qualms about discussing his private life, which is just as well, because there are lots of lessons to glean from it. It also shows that success-driven individuals and, indeed, the successful ones, are flesh and blood like us. They have struggles like us but forge ahead despite them.

Despite his professional success, Buzz's personal life did not enjoy the same glory. His mother's demise opened the door to other unsatisfactory events. He had been married for twenty-one years but had to give it all up shortly after his acclaimed journey to the moon. He got divorced from his wife.

It may have been as a result of the constraints and expectations placed on successful people, but Buzz hurriedly got married again. This time around, the union did not last more than two years. At that time, Buzz was thirty-nine years old, virile and eligible. However, he decided to take a break from marital vows and had casual relationships where things sometimes ended badly, too.

Despite his foray to the moon, Buzz always had a core with a military element. He had been a fighter pilot and had carried out sixty-six combat missions in Korea. Thus, he returned to that field after his trip to the moon. He functioned as the Commandant of the United States Air Force (USAF), but did not last long there, either.

Just like the human he was, it was not long before Buzz fell prey to the pressures all around him. He decided to seek solace in the bottle, and fell into an acute depression, gradually becoming an alcoholic. As is often the case, the alcohol first appeared to be the perfect remedy for whatever psychological and emotional ailment Buzz suffered. As is also often the case, this relief was short-lived and soon became part of the problem.

He admitted that he found it extremely arduous to share whatever he was going through with other men; in those days, men often believed they would appear weak if they admitted they were having problems. He wrote of this in his book, *Magnificient Desolation*. He could not confide in any person that his life was being torn apart, and he could barely hold it together at the seams. After everything, he retired from the service and worked as a Cadillac dealership owner in Beverly Hills, but that was also an unsuccessful endeavor. In what seemed like an outburst against the world just to vent his frustration, Buzz broke down the door to his then-girlfriend's house in a drunken state. He was arrested for this behavior.

Taking charge of his life above every other thing, he went into therapy to treat his alcoholism and came out clean after two years. He has remained sober since and has been married for approximately twenty-nine years. He served as the Chairman of National Association of Mental Health, sharing his experiences to help others.

Another icon of success who bore a great deal of trauma during his tenure as President of the United States was Abraham Lincoln. He was a victim of a severe form of clinical depression. His condition would have been questioned if he was born in our times. It is said that his parents suffered from it, and Lincoln could have inherited a propensity for it from them. Lincoln's fiancée when he was twenty-four years old, Ann Rutledge, died of an illness of non-confirmed origin. It was suspected to be typhoid, and it initiated several bouts of melancholy, although there might have been others when he was younger. He later met another lady named Mary Todd, but called off their engagement, which led to another episode of depression. Eventually, the duo tied the knot. Of the four boys he had, only one lived beyond the age of nineteen, which threw both his wife and him into depression.

Lincoln had a hard time while growing up, too. The 16th President of the United States described himself as a slave while growing up. He lost his mother at the tender age of nine. By the time he clocked twenty, the list of the family members who had died had risen to include an aunt, a sister, an uncle, and an infant brother. Lincoln also had an abusive father. Lincoln's father often used him to do odd jobs in exchange for cash.

Despite his turbulent personal life, Lincoln excelled. He sought treatment for his melancholia. Rumors then had it that the President employed even some of the most severe forms of therapies available then. He used depression as a foundation and to spur himself to do greater things for his people. He suffered from chronic depression until he was assassinated in 1865. While his life was often at loose ends, he never let it affect his country. He put an end to slavery and preserved the Union during the Civil War.

We could go on and on about the personal battles successful people fight, but we could never exhaust the list. These illustrations show that you are never alone in whatever you are going through, and it is not an excuse to give up. As turbulent as Buzz's life was, he got himself cleaned up; there is no reason that all of us cannot do the same, and more than that, as it so happens.

Personal battles are related to any personal experience that a person suffers from, which may relate to either past or present events (or both). Personal battles may be due to upbringing, health conditions, marital conditions, financial situations, and others. A personal battle can create a long-lasting impact on its host. It can impose pounds of pressure on the mind and slow down the pace of progress.

Unfortunately, not everyone understands the impact that personal battles can create. While some people are naive and cannot acknowledge their influence, some others refuse to accept the fact that they suffer from one. Meanwhile, denial is not a solution for personal battles, as it leaves a pathetic imprint on any success generated!

As turbulent as Buzz's life was, he got himself cleaned up; there is no reason that all of us cannot do the same, and more than that, as it so happens.

A personal battle can create psychological effects that wreck performances. Someone who suffers from a particular struggle may experience fear, anxiety, and depression. Of course, these are health issues that need serious medical attention. However, the impact of a personal battle is not limited to health issues only, it also affect any success attempt. An affected person is bound to lose enthusiasm for work, which will cause his production rate to dwindle.

External Pressure

Watch out for the monstrous external influences that are out there to blockade your success road trip! These factors are activities that include bullying, hostility, and peer pressure.

Bullying

Bullying is mostly associated with name-calling and undue criticism. Anyone can suffer from bullying activities. It can happen to young and old people alike. It can also happen to an individual or a group of people. Bullying activities can occur in a school environment, but they can also occur at work.

Watch out for bullies, who can be a fellow student, a coworker, or a boss. Anyone who waylays others is a bully. A boss who subjects his subordinates to undue scrutiny for whatever justification is a bully. He is a bully if he is nitpicky and micro-manages others to bolster his ego.

Bully activities can demoralize a person, creating a psychological impact that affects his work performance. No one has the right to bully others without being held accountable. As a success-aspiring person, you must exercise your right to deter any bullying activity around you. Take a stand to address your uncomfortable situation: Hold a bully responsible for his actions by reporting him to the respective authority.

Bullies have inferiority complexes, and they play pranks on others to cover up their weakness. They aim at suppressing others to appear real and have a sense of dominion. A typical bully will act to make his subject feel weak so he feels strong by comparison. As a success-minded person, you must choose to disappoint your bully by displaying an unbeatable spirit! Keep focus and maintain a mindset to achieve your goal. Also, you must take a definite step to refute the impostor of negative influences—the bully! Use all legal means to step up your defense and silence your bully.

In addition, choose to convert any destructive criticism that a bully throws at you to constructive criticism. That is, train your mind to ignore the negative connotation of a bully's comment, but seize the moment to do personal research and analysis of the speech to make the comment beneficial. Turn the comment to a source of motivation for your improvement to achieve greater success.

Hostility

A hostile environment is a cursed environment. Anyone who operates in this environment is under siege; he or she cannot perform at his best. Hostility will degrade his morale and dry up his desire for good operations and productivity.

Hostility is similar to bullying; any work environment can turn into a den of hostility when things are not put in proper perspective. That is, any improper staff behavior can degenerate into hostility in a work environment. For example, a boss who gives preferential treatment to certain staff members (at the expense of others) is creating a hostile environment. Also, a hostile environment is created when some staff members isolate an individual for any reason. They are setting a hostile stage as they limit communication and hoard beneficial information to sabotage his efforts.

Hostility can transmogrify into success road rage when leaders of an organization fail to act appropriately in due time. Consequentially, the workforce will have degraded ethics, performance, and overall efficiency.

> *Hostility is similar to bullying; any work environment can turn into a den of hostility when things are not put in proper perspective.*

Anyone who suffers from hostility should not keep silent about his situation. He must make a decisive effort to solve the problem. He can complain to the managing authority. If they fail to act, he should consider vacating the hostile environment or seeking legal intervention. Why must a person allow other people to inhibit his success exploits by constricting himself to a hostile work environment? He should look for a positive work environment and meet friendly people who are willing to offer him an unfettered chance to succeed.

Peer Pressure

Young people come to mind when the term *peer pressure* is used; however, not only young people are affected. Some adults also suffer from peer pressure. The condition is noticeable when a person operates under the influence of other people. He is forced to behave or operate in a certain way other than how he would have preferred to naturally. (This explanation does not relate to a standard operating procedure of the establishment).

Peer pressure can destroy a lifestyle; it can derail a career aspiration. A person under peer pressure is manipulated into a certain behavior or a practice that someone else introduced. Most times, the subject is manipulated to

Young people come to mind when the term peer pressure is used; however, not only young people are affected.

participate in a competition; he may also be influenced to adopt a certain lifestyle that is unrelated to his area of personal interest.

Peer pressure can be advantageous if it is properly managed. It can create motivation if a person can successfully divert the influence to an area of personal interest. Meanwhile, in spite of the benefits, peer pressure has more cons than pros. Under whatever condition, a person under the influence still runs the risk of following the wrong opinion and being subjected to participating in a rat race that leads to building a bridge that heads nowhere.

It is more advantageous to avoid peer pressure than to manage it. No need to entertain peer pressure for the sake of deriving motivation! Anyone who needs motivation to enhance his career should consider to

Peer pressure can be advantageous if it is properly managed.

receiving it from any positive source he can find. He should not consider deriving his motivation from peer pressure, which does more harm than good.

As a success-aspiring person, you must not allow anyone to push you off the cliff in the name of motivation! Be sensitive to how external factors are influencing you. Peers will mount pressure on you and claim they are helping you, but don't be fooled; they are often interested in exposing your weakness in order to bolster their egos or get ahead themselves. It's all about reverse psychology: Peers want you to compete with them in an attempt to prove how much better they are. Choose to disappoint them by making a detour. Let them run alone or look for someone else to compete with!

Don't be so egocentric as to try to impress anyone on your success road trip. People who do so are trapped into seeking personal approval. The victims are also trapped into running rat races that contribute little or nothing to their aspirations. Believe in your dream and run it with common sense! Don't allow your peers to make you live in their dreams. You have the right to reject any idea that does not align with your dream.

Live your life purposefully by only accepting an adventure or a business proposal that relates to your aspirations. Turn down irrelevant offers and be on your way to achieving great success in life!

Society Myths

The culture a person grows up in can dictate how he conducts his business. He has natural traits that is similar to his local friends; he also has tendency to engage in similar business and operate in the same way. Meanwhile, the system of operating common business with common practices often yields limited success, since the environment would have become saturated. A person who wants to have a significant breakthrough must venture not to follow the trend of *common-man business*. Either he engages in a similar business and operates differently, or he engages in a completely different type of business that will help him excel.

A success-conscious person must *think outside of the box* by engaging in prospective rare businesses with the use of unique implementation techniques. He must do all he can to avoid going with the flow a cultural practice that has already proven to be nonproductive.

A typical status quo business practice offers meager rewards. A person who has the right perspective must think differently and be creative. He must do research and aim to acquire knowledge from other beneficial

> *A person who wants to have a significant breakthrough must venture not to follow the trend of common-man business.*

sources. Some good business ideas can be derived from literature. A person who reads the right book will gain knowledge that is applicable to his work. Also, a person can derive many benefits from an academic arena if an appropriate field of study is selected. Those relevant courses will steer his mind into creativity and also enhance his ability to task his mind into developing a prospective system of practice.

Road Rage Solution

Road rage factors lead to poor work performance, low productivity, and low profit margins. No success-aspiring person should be complacent regarding these factors. A person ought to attempt to solve problems and influence those he can't solve to tilt positively to his advantage.

Some road rage factors can be addressed, but some others have complex origins that are not easily tackled. A person affected should consult the experts who are trained to handle the respective problems. Meanwhile, as the person

> *Road rage factors lead to poor work performance, low productivity, and low profit margins.*

affected with road rage factors seeks solutions, he must bear in mind that the results may not bring an absolute solution. Some problems are complex and cannot be solved in an instant; therefore, a person who is conscious about success must not wait for an ideal situation to formulate before he makes proper efforts to forge ahead with his aspirations. The person can derive motivation from the following listed statements:

➢ The world is not perfect, and no one is problem-free. Everyone has one issue or the other he needs to resolve. Life must move on.

➢ The fact that a problem arose doesn't mean the end has come. The world still continues, and folks who navigate around their odds will succeed.

➤ The future will remain promising for anyone who keeps his hope afloat.

➤ A person who is determined can dominate his problems and break free into a solution.

A success-aspiring person must understand that life is not friendly to anyone. Meanwhile, despite the unfriendly situations that life presents, a few folks have proven to be unstoppable. They have developed a thick skin to refute challenges. They are also able to develop skill-sets that are suitable to aid them to rebound from any failure. These folks have the ability to fight their odds; they can carve success out of any unpalatable situation.

> *A success-aspiring person must understand that life is not friendly to anyone.*

Key Points

➤ Successful people also have troubles of their own that can stem from marital problems, financial insecurity, and a host of other factors.

➤ Success comes with inevitable pressures from the external world, which are more noticeable in our day than ever.

➤ Bullies have no other job description than to criticize. It is never enjoyable and should not be tolerated. Make your stand known and confront your bullies. If you do not do that, you will have to endure them for the rest of your life.

➤ If you find yourself in a hostile environment, speak out for yourself. No one can perform at the optimum level in a hostile place. It is a poison that seeps into the blood.

➤ Although peer pressure affects the young more than any other group, no one is entirely immune to it.

➤ Do not wait to manage peer pressure and avoid it if you can.

➤ There are societal myths that are limiting factors. The way out is to challenge them. There can be no great reward for keeping your creativity captive because the society does not support it. Dare to be different!

➤ Regardless of disappointments, do not let anyone stop you from pursuing your success.

THE MYTH OF SUCCESS

It is bad decision to BLINDLY follow any religion.

Immortal Technique

While many controversies surround the story of Galileo, a fervent believer of the theory of Nicholas Copernicus, there is one thing that stands out and cannot be debated. The Roman Catholic Church resisted the theory of heliocentrism, the belief that the earth rotates around its axis and revolves around the sun. The general opinion then was geocentrism, that the Earth was the center of the solar system. This case is an example of religious dictates forcing others to follow certain ideologies and refusing to consider other options.

Not all people appreciate the pursuit of success; some individuals, religious and secular, consider it against their beliefs to have success-related discussions, let alone pursue it for themselves. They argue that people are not born equal, and not everyone can succeed. Some folks just have to remain poor for others to be rich, they claim. Consequentially, these folks, who take a rare stand against the pursuit of success, end up living in poverty. Since they already have the poverty mindset, their drive for success becomes distorted. Therefore, they are unable to realize their aspirations, or simply don't have any.

Religious individuals who reject the pursuit of success find it difficult to act out of the ordinary. They tend to be complacent with their ideology. The only thing they do is to pray and wait for God's miracles to happen. Unfortunately, these people may soon experience disappointment, because God does not support laziness. While the Creator expects His children to exercise faith, He also wants them to be diligent workers. God himself is a hard worker who shared the same attribute with humanity when He created the first man and woman.

Success won't drop from the sky on anyone's lap. God wants everyone to utilize his naturally given resources to generate success. The Miracle Worker will favor whoever diligently invests his resources, including physical and intellectual abilities. That is, a person of faith will have God's blessing if he can activate his resources and put them to good use! Those resources were already wired into his system during the Creation.

> *Success won't drop from the sky on anyone's lap. God wants everyone to utilize his naturally given resources to generate success.*

Every man (and woman) must respond to the call of his or her God to explore the Earth and have success. Each person must make *hard work* his routine exercise, without letting a religion block his success roadmap.

No matter the type of religion a person adopts and the level of faith he has attained, he ought to consider that he was created to make a good use of his gifts and be successful. As a religious person, he should consider himself to have an advantage over others, since he can derive success motivation from his faith.

People who stay idle, hoping to receive God's blessing, should be expecting to receive nothing in return. God hates laziness; He loves diligence! He is principled, and everything He does goes by His principles. The Creator cannot violate His own rule to bless lazy people. Therefore, anyone who anticipates God's blessing should diligently engage in his (or her) business!

Anyone who wants to have success in his lifetime must abide by the principle of *hard work* that God himself operates with! He worked so hard during creation that He was exhausted and needed to rest on the Seventh Day! Hence, a man must get busy with his unique ability to explore the Earth for his beneficial use and for his success.

A person who has been blaming God for a lack of success should reorient himself to stop the blame game. If he genuinely wants to succeed, he must change his mindset to embrace the fact that God created everyone to succeed in life. God never outsources failure; neither does he cause anyone to fail! A success-aspiring person must tap himself to be proactive in making a good use of his resources to achieve his

> *God hates laziness; He loves diligence! He is principled, and everything He does goes by His principles.*

anticipated success. (You may read a related blog post about this subject here: *www.bit.ly/diligent-children*)

Key Points

➢ A man's religion can inhibit his work performance if he believes in wrongful ideologies. He will lose the sense of excitement and be unable to make good use of any available resources he has.

➢ People who believe all people are not born equally to succeed will lack the drive needed to pursue their aspirations. They will live in poverty.

➢ God is a hard worker; he shared his attributes with humanity. Therefore, a man must work hard to have success.

➢ Principles rule the world. Even God works by them and upholds them.

➢ Poverty is not equivalent to religion.

➢ People who stay idle and hope to receive God's blessing should be expecting to receive nothing in return. God hates laziness.

➢ Don't blame God for your failure; blame yourself!

➢ God does not promote laziness; he doesn't want a person to avoid his responsibility and hope to receive a divine blessing.

> ➤ If you keep praying continuously and have your hands folded without putting them to work, poverty is knocking on your door.
>
> ➤ God wants us to be successful.

HOW YOUR PAST
AFFECTS YOUR FUTURE

Some of the best lessons we ever learned are from past mistakes. The error of the past is the wisdom and success of the future.

Dale Turner

There was a young and wealthy rider who owned a horse. He loved his horse very much and held it close to his heart. He would wake up in the morning and tend to the needs of the animal. The hay and water never ran out in the stable. Often, he gave the horse a treat by feeding it bits of sugar. There was a strong bond between man and beast. On a particular day, he went on a journey that took him through the jungle. Due to the peculiarity of the terrain, the night fell while they were still in the wooded area.

The horse could not see well as a result of canopies covering whatever little light was still available and fell into a ditch. The young man was sad, as he could not leave his companion in this uncomfortable position. There was no one around to help, even though he shouted until he lost his voice. Gearing himself up, he attempted to drag the horse out but to no avail. After several failed trials, he decided to continue on his journey because he could not bear to look at the animal in such pitiable condition.

However, as the last show of kindness, he decided to give the horse a befitting burial by covering it with sand. As soon as he poured the dirt, the animal would dust off its body and climb on the discarded dirt. Gradually, he began to use it as leverage. When the owner realized this, he poured the sand with more vigor, and in no time, man and beast were reunited. The horse used the dirt thrown at him as a ladder to climb out of the ditch.

A person's past can influence his present life. That is, an experience, whether negative or positive, and irrespective of any fact that it maimed or made a person, can derail his success exploits. Anyone who intends to make advancement in his or her success lane must not allow the past to double cross him or her. If he does, he is more or less a driver who attempts to accelerate his vehicle in the reverse gear. He won't reach his anticipated destination.

A dreamer of success must disengage from his past to have his dream comes true. He must encourage himself to declare, "The past has passed, my life must move forward."

Anyone who realizes that he makes sporadic achievements in his success lane should question himself to determine whether he is a victim of some experience in the past or not. Perhaps he is suffering from some past influences that he needs to dissociate from. Does the person frequently reflect on his past to entertain self-pity? Is he overly excited about his recent achievements and reflect on them at all times? If a response to any of the two questions is affirmative, then he is a victim. The person is operating under the shadow of his past; he must take a corrective action, or else his success wheels will drag.

> *Anyone who intends to make advancement in his or her success lane must not allow the past to double cross him or her.*

It is not entirely wrong to reflect on the past. Someone can reflect on it to benefit his present life and the future. Also, he can reflect on his past and learn from it to become a better person. However, everything goes wrong when the reflection of history does not generate success motivation. The past must not be allowed to influence the present and the future negatively.

A person affected (positively or negatively) by the past must get to a point where he detaches his mind and allows a fresh influx of prospects and knowledge. The practice of consistently dwelling on an experience will result in *brain drain*. It will

Everything goes wrong when the reflection of history does not generate success motivation. The past must not be allowed to influence the present and the future negatively.

shortchange the mind to be blindsided. He will not be able to see or reckon with future opportunities. A mind affected will perform poorly and be unable to adequately explore any available resources. Of course, this will dwindle his productivity rate.

A person whose past was sweet should derive motivation from it to make necessary success progress. Instead of getting overly excited about the history and become complacent, he should turn the experience into a launching pad for new creativity. He should turn his lesson learned from the previous achievement into making a new forecast that will earn him more success.

Anyone whose past was bitter or sour should learn and disengage from it. He cannot indefinitely dwell on his experience and expect to have a prospective future. The situation may be unfortunate, but the person must be courageous enough to keep his dream alive and active. He must be working toward achieving his goal despite any horrific memory he has sustained. The past may be irreversible, but the future has plenty of opportunities to offer. Therefore, the affected person must not live with self-pity or be forever remorseful! He should summon the courage to keep advancing his dream until it comes true.

It is essential that a person who is haunted by a horrific experience make every necessary effort to detach from it. Otherwise, he will not have anything significant to write home about. No other choice than for him to detach. He must attempt to run; if he can't run, he should walk. If he feels walking is not possible, then he should crawl! He must be determined to do something that will make his life progressive, no matter the circumstance.

Deal with Your Past

Human memory cannot be wiped clean of a horrific past, but it can be trained to overcome it. A person who wants to improve his status should not attempt a quick-fix for any problem. He should consider dealing with it once and for all, but seriously. An attempt to casually deal with a horrible past has proven to be unproductive; the feelings will gather again and resurface! Also, an attempt to deny or suppress any sustained psychological impact is counterproductive. The painful memory will resurface to haunt the affected person; the aftermath effect may even be more complicated.

> *Human memory cannot be wiped clean of a horrific past, but it can be trained to overcome it.*

95

It is important that a person prepares his mind and is ready to deal with his horrific past when he attempts a solution. Otherwise, the effort may fully open up an old wound and create more damage. The person should consider taking the following steps when he is fully prepared to deal with a painful past:

1. Label the horrific experience with a specific title, which may be abuse, disappointment, loss, or trauma, or something else.

2. Identify the person that you believe is responsible for the situation. This can be you or someone else.

3. Mention the impact that the situation has made in your life. The effect may have been on your education, finance, health, relationship, or other.

4. State how you have reacted to the situation.

5. Let off the weight of the horrific experience by declaring your new stand.

6. If you are responsible for the heinous situation, state, "I have forgiven myself."

7. If someone else is responsible for the situation, mention his or her name and state, "I have forgiven (mention the person's name)."

8. Verbalize your new stand to have it register in your mind. State, "From now on, I will not allow my past to affect

An attempt to deny or suppress any sustained psychological impact is counterproductive.

me anymore. My past has passed, and from now on, I will move on with my life."

9. Consult a professional counselor or a psychologist for an event or a situation that you cannot personally handle.

Fight Challenges to Win Success

A person who aims for success must fight in life to achieve it. Why? Life is all about battle! It does not present its goodies on a platter of gold. Life has to be rough-handled before it can release its substantial benefits. For anyone to successfully fight and win life, he has to be defiant to any negative circumstance around him.

No one is immune to life challenges. They intrude and toss lives around; however, not all challenges are destructive. Some challenges are blessing in disguise, and they will become beneficial if they are properly handled. A challenge can be an effective tool of success if it is handled properly.

A success-aspiring person must be careful not to lay too much emphasis on the negative influence of his circumstances. He should see something beneficial on both sides of the coin that life tosses for him. He should let his problem inspire him to be more determined in his pursuit of success. To achieve this, he must be careful

The mind perceives a challenge as a temporary circumstance that needs to be addressed at a fast rate. The mind perceives a problem as a prominent negative circumstance that requires much energy.

not to be too quick in labeling any issue a problem. Rather, he should refer to it as a challenge. Why? Both problem and challenge have negative connotations, but not in a similar fashion.

The mind perceives and reacts to each of them differently. The mind perceives a challenge as a temporary circumstance that needs to be addressed at a fast rate. The mind perceives a problem as a prominent negative circumstance that requires much energy.

A person who intends to transform his odds to success should attempt the following steps:

1. Be inclined to always label a tough situation as a "Challenge" rather than calling it a "Problem."

The word "Problem" imposes the feeling of a pronounced negative influence, which can overwhelm the mind and discourage it to find a formidable solution. In contrast, the word "Challenge" carries a mild negative connotation, which the mind perceives to be temporary, thereby reacting quickly to resolve it.

2. Analyze the factors that surround your odds.

A difficult situation may have some other fragmented negative factors attached. The process of obtaining a solution may have to include those subsidiaries. In some cases, the fragmented factors have to be completely resolved before the predominant situation is corrected.

3. Evaluate your options before exploring for a solution.

Don't rush into attacking your challenge once you have identified it. Carefully weigh your options before you act. An instant suggested solution that pops into your mind may not be the real solution you need. Consider the gravity of your options; evaluate them to know which one might create a significant ripple effect that yields lasting solution.

Take Advantage of Your Problem

As a success-aspiring person, you must choose to turn your adversity into achievement. You may have to do some research and map out options that can help you navigate around your odds to activate your untapped opportunity. The means justifies the end; your efforts invested in refuting a challenge will eventually pay the dividend.

Life has never been fair to anyone. It won't present its opportunity to you on a platter of gold; therefore, you cannot be complacent with a restricted lifestyle. Fight your odds to make life tilt its scale of success to your side. In some cases, adversity may be what you need to have success. As you resist the trouble, your muscles will build and sustain success characteristics.

> *Life has never been fair to anyone. It won't present its opportunity to you on a platter of gold; therefore, you cannot be complacent with a restricted lifestyle.*

As a success-aspiring person, you can't afford to be complacent with your situation and be claiming life is unfair. You must be responsive to your location and make your negative situation turn positive.

The rule of adversity as it relates to success proves that any stressful situation pulls success to the surface, and also encourages a person to exercise his critical thinking ability. That is, adversity forces people to think deeper and be proactive in getting any needed solution. As the person persists in resisting the hardship, the more increased intrinsic value will formulate, which will ultimately help him to have sound success.

Consider this: If you swing your bat once and hit a ball, will you need to make further attempts? No. In contrast, if you aim and miss your target, your brain will trigger a hormone necessary to make you train and retry the process until you can finally get it right. Your initial failure wasn't a problem; it was a challenge that imposed the need to take further action that unveils your athletic capability, an opportunity you may never have had if you had hit a home run in your first attempt.

> *The rule of adversity as it relates to success proves that any stressful situation pulls success to the surface.*

Key Points

- ➢ Past experiences, whether positive or negative, can drag the wheels of success. None of the two is inert. There will always be an effect.
- ➢ A dreamer of success must disengage from his past to have his dream come true.
- ➢ A person who perpetually lives in self-pity or remorse is a prisoner of his past.

➢ It is not entirely wrong to reflect on an experience. Someone can reflect on his past to benefit his present life and the future. You must produce something positive from the thoughts.

➢ Anyone who wants his dream to come true must dissociate from his negative past at all costs.

➢ He cannot wipe his memory of his horrific past, but he can train his mind to stop dwelling on it.

➢ An attempt to casually deal with a horrible past is counterproductive, since the problem will resurface again, and in some cases, the issue may even be more complicated. Take steps to deal with your past.

➢ Some challenges can be beneficial. They can become effective tools of success if they are properly handled.

➢ The human mind moves faster to resolve a challenge than to react to a problem. The mind lightly esteems a challenge but considers a problem to be a dominant situation that needs more energy.

➢ The brain tends to resolve a "challenge" faster than it would respond to a "problem."

➢ Don't rush into a conclusion about a challenge you confront, and don't rush into making a quick decision until you have carefully weighed your options.

➢ Life has never been fair to anyone. It won't present its opportunity to you on a platter of gold; therefore, you cannot be complacent with a restricted lifestyle. Fight your odds to make life tilt the scale of success to your side.

GOAL PLANNING AND BENEFITS

Our goals can only be reached through a vehicle of a plan, in which we must fervently believe, and upon which we must vigorously act. There is no other route to success.

Pablo Picasso

Marie is a single mother of three children, two boys and a girl. She is a Marketing Executive in a Fortune 500 bank with a crazy schedule. Her busy work plan and career choice demand that she is mostly out of the house. She runs a restaurant, too. With three sectors of her life demanding so much more from her than she can manage, she is completely losing it. She is on the verge of a nervous breakdown, and she knows it has to stop. The signs are all there, but she is perplexed on how to go about fixing things. Aside from organizing her life, she also needs to rest her body.

Marie was still in this rut when she met Stephanie, her childhood friend. They had drifted apart after graduating from the high school. Each person had gone on to pursue what interested her. Stephanie was a doctor with a crazy schedule as well. She also had her business of knitting. She did a double-take when she saw her friend at the mall, because she was not sure if it was her. The Marie she knew was not as old or tired-looking as the person standing before her. She decided to approach her and ask where she could be of help.

Stephanie discovered that her friend was under much stress not because of anything but a lack of organization. She wanted to do so much more at once than she could manage. She had targets and deadlines to meet at work; she had a business to oversee and three beautiful children to handle. Her boys were already showing some wild

> *The problem with failure is summed up in this saying: People never plan to fail, they fail to plan.*

traits due to peer pressure, which added to her culminating stressors. Marie was on the path to success, but everything could come undone if things were not done according to the principles of success. What is the way out of her rut?

Stephanie had been like Marie some years back until she learned the essence of organization and planning. She had to teach her friend, or she would break under the pressure.

The problem with failure is summed up in this saying: People never plan to fail, they fail to plan.

"But don't begin until you count the cost. For who would begin construction of a building without first getting estimates and then checking to see if he has enough money to pay the bills? Otherwise he might complete only

> *The lack of an adequate plan can cause a person to incessantly juggle unimportant activities and wind up wasting the energy he needs to tackle the tasks that are important.*

the foundation before running out of funds. And then how everyone would laugh!" (Luke 14:28-29 TLB)

Any typical project consists of various activities, which can turn cumbersome when proper planning is not put in place. The lack of an adequate plan can cause a person to incessantly juggle unimportant activities and wind up wasting the energy he needs to tackle the tasks that are important. Inadequate planning can also affect operational flow. It leads to a delay of schedules. A venturer runs the risk of keeping a backlog of essential project activities; thereby negatively influencing the overall success rate. Indeed, a lack of adequate planning can be destructive to any prospective aspiration! Learn from Bob's illustration below and be sure not to be like him.

Bob lives in NY and loves to run. He needed a wrench to fix his broken toilet pipe. He heard the wrench is only available in Chicago. Therefore, he put on his athletic shoes and started running. He took him a journey of three weeks to reach Chicago. On getting there, he was told that the store had been relocated to NY. The new place was the street next to Bob's house! Thus, he had to make a return trip to where he came from anyway. What a sheer waste! Bob wasted time and money because his feet were running faster than his mind. The lesson here is that you need to think before you act.

Goal-planning offers the benefit of staying focused on the work within the scope of a pre-defined operation. It will help to minimize the chances of getting distracted and making irrational decisions. As you embark on the project, fresh ideas will pop into your mind. However, because of the plan already crafted ahead of time, you will remain focused and complete the task undistracted. Of course, there is no harm in having new ideas, but they should not be permitted to cause

> *Goal-planning offers the benefit of staying focused on the work within the scope of a pre-defined operation.*

106

a distraction from the current work. They should be saved for a later project or date.

A person who plans well has the advantage to sort his activities and prioritize them to have a productive result. He or she can make a proper evaluation of his work to determine whether he is making progress or not. The performance evaluation will also help him to know his areas of strengths and weaknesses. Better still, a person who plans has an advantage of running a smooth operation without suffering from any unnecessary hiccups. He can keep the flow and pace of his activities to meet deadlines. If the work continues to progress in this manner, success is within reach!

A person who plans his tasks can earn himself an opportunity to enhance his creative ability.

Goal planning can help a person to complete his tasks ahead of schedule. The mind has a chance to master the sequence of activities. Therefore, it can efficiently operate at a fast rate to generate results. Also, a person who plans his tasks can earn himself an opportunity to enhance his creative ability. Since his mind would be less busy perform its functions, it will become inclined to receiving a fresh inflow of ideas that can boost the prospect of his work.

The Importance of a To-Do List in Goal Setting

The to-do list is a tool that creates a clear pathway for task implementation. Every success admirer ought to explore the use of this accessory in driving his goal for meeting success expectations. The making of a to-do list is not difficult. The task requires no particular skill; anyone can benefit from it. However, despite the simplicity of its creation, many people still do not explore the use of a to-do list to run their operations. Some folks who consider its importance also have a problem to keep up with its use. They soon abandon any agenda they make and revert to their routine of juggling between multiple tasks. Unfortunately, these people end up getting trapped. They apply their resources to irrelevant activities while the important ones remain untouched.

Others do not fall into the category mentioned above; they just doubt any beneficial use of a to-do list. They presume that it will restrict their operations and lead to a waste of time. However, the reverse is the case. People who refuse to appreciate the importance of a to-do list may claim they are brilliant enough to memorize

Only a robot has a perfect memory, based on how it is programmed. The human mind has a limited capability.

all activities that are related to their task. However, their claim can't be validated! Only a robot has a perfect memory, based on how it is programmed. The human mind has a limited capability. It can suffer a memory lag or memory loss. Humans can only retain specific information for some time, after which it will slowly fade and vanish. How? The steady and unrestricted inflow of new information will force the brain to move an existing item from an active mode to a passive one. It is then archived. The information stored would only become active when it is recalled for a particular need. If that does not take place for a long time, it will fade in the archive and eventually have a slow death.

A to-do list will help anyone to successfully keep the pace and maintain an operation frequency that can meet a target goal without experiencing any memory malfunctioning. A to-do list applies to every aspect of life. It is useful for making great exploits that relate to purchases, education, finances, investment, and others. A to-do list can be used to meet day-to-day needs. It can also be utilized to achieve long-term goals. Despite the various purposes of a to-do list, only one universal approach is needed to keep it active and productive. Any to-do list that is considered productive must meet the following criteria:

- ➢ It must have a definite tone.

- ➢ It must be rational.

- ➢ It must have priorities set.

- ➢ It must have checks and balances.

- ➢ It must be sortable.

- ➢ It must be time-specific.

As said earlier, you do not need any unique skill to make a to-do list. Only a pen and paper are required! Also, in this digital age, people have the opportunity to make a useful to-do list with computers and mobile devices. Some free mobile applications have come handy for this purpose. The making of a to-do list does not require any special education or technical know-how. A person can be clueless about technical expertise and still operate an effective to-do list. If he can read and write, then he can make a good to-do list and benefit from it! Anyone who is concerned about how to initiate a to-do list should grab a pen and a notepad to start jotting down whatever comes to his mind as it relates to his work. That is, he needs not to bother about any special formatting; he can start anyway. An elementary stage of a to-do list is usually rough. It will lack structure and miss some bells and whistles of success. You should not bother about those details, since they can be added later.

It is vital that a person who attempts to make a to-do list does not place a priority on style at the initial stage. He shouldn't be obsessed with the structure, either. Instead, he should centralize his effort on adding all necessary activities to his list. The startup stage (whether rough or not) will lay the groundwork that can be later improved and polished to meet standard expectation.

A to-do list can be classified into three categories, which are unsorted to-do list, sorted to-do list, and master to-do list.

Unsorted To-Do List

An unsorted to-do list is more or less a draft list that needs improvement to meet a specific expectation. It offers the groundwork for establishing a prospective list. An unsorted to-do list does not have rules in place. It may contain any project-related item without honoring the state of orderliness. An example of an unsorted to-do list is given below.

- Submit new contract proposal to A-Z Company

- Meet an accountant

- Send out memorandum to staff members

- Reset database passcode

- Make a follow-up call to a new client

- Submit payment requisition for completed contract

Sorted To-Do List

A sorted to-do list has the bells and whistles of success. It carries information that provides a clear pathway for meeting any targeted goal. The sorted to-do list solves the problem of randomness. The list items are arranged to allow a smooth operation. The following list is an example of a sorted to-do list, which was developed from the previous version.

- Submit new contract proposal to A-Z Company on Monday

morning

- Meet an accountant on Tuesday afternoon

- Send out memorandum to staff members on Wednesday morning

- Reset database passcode on Thursday afternoon

- Make a follow-up call to a new client on Friday morning

- Submit payment requisition to Lions Company on Friday afternoon

Master To-Do List

A master to-do list can be referred to as "a mission agenda." It's an advanced version of the sorted to-do list that has finishing touches and a chronological order. The master to-do list has a date and time indicated for each list item. On some occasions, and depending on the project type, a master to-do list can also have a person assigned to the specific list item. The master to-do list grants an operation supervisor a sense of security that a project will be performed efficiently. He can foresee the prospect from the get-go, because each list item has the specificity of time and an assigned individual to complete it. Here is an example of a master to-do list that is developed from the previous sorted list.

- Direct Mr. George to submit new contract proposal to A-Z Company on Monday at 10AM

- Meet Ms. Lisa - the company accountant - on Tuesday at 1PM

- Email the company's new policy memorandum to all staff members on Wednesday at 11AM

- Reset database passcode on Thursday at 2PM

- Make a follow-up call to Mr. Smith - a new client - on Friday at 10AM

- Submit payment requisition to Lions Company on Friday at 3PM

Priority rules the world of a to-do list! Both the sorted and master to-do lists must have the rule of priority factored into their development. The scale of preference brings operational effectiveness. It helps a person to make an efficient use of his time, energy, and other resources. That is, the person who runs the list will have an opportunity to exert his resources of fresh energy and others to an area where they are most needed before getting exhausted. Also, assigning priority will help a person to arrange his activities according to their level of importance. He can rank the most important action at the top of the list and make any related others its subsidiary.

The following rules must apply to any to-do list that is considered productive:

Rule No.1

A to-do list must be simple to understand.

A to-do list must consist of simple terms for easy understanding. A to-do list is neither a book nor a booklet. The list items must never be described in paragraph format! The list must only contain bullet points of actions to be taken. Also, a person who makes a to-do list must be careful to transcribe his thoughts into written words with the consciousness of not using complex terminology. That is, the list should not require consultation of a dictionary before it can be comprehended.

Rule No.2

A to-do list must be actively visited and be updated.

There must be a consistent schedule on when a to-do list is used. For example, if it is developed for weekly operation, it must be consulted on the first day of the week and be revised on the last day of the week. That is, it must be updated at the close of the last business day of each week and be operation-ready for the week following.

Rule No.3

The priority level of each list item must be honored.

Consistency is needed to operate a to-do list. A person who operates it must be disciplined to keep the chronology order and honor the priority level of each item. He can't violate the sequence and swerve for random implementation. He must stick to the list and maintain the operational flow to keep the momentum that will make a targeted goal be achieved within the time estimated. Also, following the priority of each list item will help a person to complete his essential activities on time, and avoid running into the risk of a task postponement.

Rule No.4

Only one list item must be tackled at a time.

A person who operates a to-do list must focus on performing a single list item and pretend there are no other to-do items. He must stay focused to bring the task to a completion with an undivided attention. He can only ponder other list items after the activity at stake has been fully completed.

Key Points

➢ Never begin anything until you have counted the cost. If you don't count your costs, you may have to stop the project midway.

➢ No matter how tempted you are to act, remember to think thoroughly first.

➢ Goal planning saves you time and resources. People suffer unimaginable losses for not allocating adequate time to thorough planning. Most people do not fully understand the importance of planning until they start reaping its benefits.

➢ Employ the benefits of a to-do-list to organize your day-to-day activities.

➢ The contents of your list are more important than the style or structure.

➢ Prioritize your work. The essentials should come first on the Scale of Preference.

➢ There are mainly three types of to-do-lists, namely: unsorted to-do list, sorted to-do list, and master to-do list.

➢ The unsorted to-do-list is just as the name implies— unsorted. The items on it are written in no particular order of preference. It is a draft to jog the memory on things that need to be done.

> The sorted to-do-list goes further to include a measure of orderliness and the urgency of the actions. It sends a message to the brain on the importance of the items and how to approach the day.

> The master to-do-list is the heart of success. It does not just consider orderliness and urgency; it gives a time constraint as well. Thus, the user knows just how important each task is, and when and where it must be executed.

> Just like the concept of success, the to-do-list has some rules that must be considered to be effective. They are: Simplicity, Activeness, Prioritization, and a Plan to tackle one item at a time.

HOW TO SET AN EFFECTIVE GOAL

A goal properly set is halfway reached.

Zig Ziglar

Samantha finally met with her aunt. It had been ages, but now she knew her business idea didn't need to die silently anymore. After visiting several banks and getting turned down, she had given up her plans to start a business. She worked at a radio station, but it wasn't a typical 9-5 job, and she felt she could handle more. She only worked for a few hours a day. She knew that a business would help her in achieving her dreams; hence her quest. Now she was with her aunt, Britt (a business mogul) and she was sure to come up with a solution.

Britt asked Samantha a couple of questions and realized that the younger lady didn't know the exact kind of goods she wanted to sell. Samantha knew she wanted to have a store but hadn't decided on what she would like to sell, she had no time frame in which she hoped to start the business, and she hadn't spoken with anyone who owns a store. On further questioning, Britt realized that her niece had no idea on how having a store (where she sold stuff) would have a greater effect on her dream of running a textile company later on. No wonder several banks had refused her a loan.

From this story, Samantha thought she was making enough effort to make her dreams come true, but she hadn't even started. Just like Samantha, many dreamers are out there who are not making enough effort to make their dreams come true. Unfortunately, goals set haphazardly don't reward people. They have to be properly set, brought into materialization and be appropriately implemented before any success can be achieved. Proper factors have to be put into perspective before an anticipated success can be made. Any goal considered as prospective must fit the SMART acronym (Doran, G. T. (1981). "There's a S.M.A.R.T. Way to Write Management's Goals and Objectives", Management Review, Vol. 70, Issue 11, pp. 35-36). The goal must be Specific, Measurable, Achievable, Realistic, and Timely. Only then, can its implementation be a successful one.

The SMART Rule

SPECIFIC:

A goal considered to be prospective must have a clear description. It must have a specific target to meet or answer. A goal can't be loosely described. The descriptive terminologies must be specific and be simple for easy comprehension for any interested party. It must literally hit the nail on the head. Anybody who takes a look at your written goal must be able to fully grasp the concept; even in your absence. The following two simple examples emphasize the difference between explicit and nonspecific goals.

Example 1

Nonspecific goal: *"I want to open a retail store"*

Specific goal: **"I want to open a plus-size women's clothing retail store"**

Example 2

Nonspecific goal: *"I want to save some money by end of this year."*

Specific goal: **"I want to save $2,000 by end of this year."**

MEASURABLE:

A goal expected to be successful must have a measurement. It must have a clear path on how to meet an objective, which must be properly monitored. It must have accountability, which includes a start-to-finish timeframe, quantity, quality, cost, and frequency. That is, a measurable goal must be trackable to help a dreamer determine if he is making proper progress. Without this concept, the dreamer will roam about on the same spot for a long time and make no timely progress. A diary, computer software, or mobile application can be used to meet this requirement.

Example

Unmeasurable goal: *"By the end of the lesson, I should know mathematics."*

Measurable goal: **"By the end of the class, I should know how to solve word problems using algebra."**

ACHIEVABLE:

A goal considered to be prospective must be achievable. Its description must be at least somewhat realistic. Its description can't consist of an uncertain promise; it must be crystal clear with a definite tone. The goal must be perceived to be within reach. Also, the scope of operation must be within the available resources. In short, an achievable goal must be inclusive of the following assets:

> *Personal ability is an essential rung on the ladder to success!*

1. Skill ability

2. Resources availability

3. Time availability

Example

Unachievable goal: *"My new year resolution is to improve my writing skill and publish a new book every month."*

Achievable goal: ***"My new year resolution is to finish the first draft of my book by March 31st, complete the editing process by May 1st, and complete design and publishing by June 31st."***

Personal ability is an essential rung on the ladder to success! A person who aims to make his goal achievable must venture to develop his capacity and bring it to an entirely operational display. Personal ability comes in different shapes and forms: Reading, writing, speech, and a host of other individual skills can contribute to success. Of these skills, a few are very important. Every prospective venturer must have them at disposal! One unique example to consider here is critical thinking ability. A venturer must have this skill to weather turbulence and maintain balance as he aspires to drive his goal toward fulfillment.

Critical thinking will help a venturer to address any unforeseen circumstance as he works on actualizing his goal. The person can envision what's in the future and plan for it at the same time. He can presume if any part of his plan will work or not. He can solve a difficult problem and can make an alternate path for any problem that proves unsolvable. The skill of critical thinking *can be learned* and developed, especially if a person is committed to the course.

> *Critical thinking will help a venturer to address any unforeseen circumstance as he works on actualizing his goal.*

RELEVANT:

A goal worth pursuing must be relevant to the overall mission of the venturer. It cannot come out of the blue, and it can't be run because it merely appears to be promising. It must really be promising. The goal in pursuit must answer the question "Why?" It must meet the mandate of satisfying an overall objective of the venturer. Hence, it is important for the venturer to draw this goal from a bigger picture (his overall objective). Also, the prospective impact of the goal must be evaluated to achieve certain success threshold.

Example

Irrelevant goal: *"I aspire to be a civil engineer, so I will select my major classes in the performing arts."*

Relevant goal: ***"I aspire to be a civil engineer, so I will select my major classes in building construction and management."***

TIMELY:

Timeliness will offer a venturer the benefit of making his project meet a specific deadline. Each activity must have a particular time (and date) assigned to it to achieve this goal. The specificity of time will guide the venturer to track his work progress. Procrastination can set in if there are no time limits. With set time limits, he can easily determine if an estimated completion date is feasible or not. This will earn him the benefit of rearranging his goals to meet his overall expectations.

Example

Untimely: *"I want to publish my first business book this year."*

Timely: **"I want to publish my first business book this year. Here is my breakdown:**

- **I will finish my first draft by March 31st**

- **I will complete the editing process by May 1st**

- **I will complete the book design by June 30st**

- **I will publish and launch the book on July 31st"**

Poor timing inhibits the goal implementation process. A venturer has the responsibility to manage his time to meet success expectation adequately. Pressure will be mounted on him to complete many tasks at the same time. He must be disciplined enough not to engage in any activity that can cause him to trade quantity for quality! Irrespective of the pressure he faces, he must make sure to have quality product available at the delivery time.

An adventurer who multitasks in the hope of saving some time runs the risk of losing the quality of his work! He has a high chance of substituting quantity for quality as he incessantly juggles between multiple tasks. To solve this problem, the person must discipline himself to keep to his original work schedule. He must not allow any unnecessary activity influence or interrupt the progress of his work. The person

> *An adventurer who multitasks in the hope of saving some time runs the risk of losing the quality of his work!*

should only consider amending his schedule to meet an emergency situation, which of course is not expected to happen at all times! If a plan is frequently interrupted by an emergency situation, then the adventurer should consider revising it to have a practical implementation process.

Key Points

➤ Setting goals in a careless manner yields nothing tangible.

➤ Only meticulously set goals and their implementation yield the massive success we desire.

➤ Factors to be put under consideration in goal setting are described by the "SMART" acronym. A goal should be Smart, Measurable, Achievable, Realistic and Timely.

➤ Expected success is associated with goals that are explicit in their description.

➤ Work out a way to be accountable to your goals per time. They can even be tracked using your technological gadgets.

➤ The definition of your goal should be clear and certain.

➤ Your goal should have a part to play in the larger picture of your life's mission.

➤ Deadlines help to keep progress in check and avoid procrastination.

THE REALITY OF GOAL IMPLEMENTATION

Intention without action is an insult to those who expect the best from you.

Andy Andrews

In a Kingdom that existed long before now, a King once had a daughter. He had many sons as well, but he loved no one as much as he loved the girl. Although the tradition was that the first son would become the King after the demise of the King or anytime he felt he cannot continue, he had no intention of following that tradition. He made sure that he provided everything his daughter desired. She only had to name it, and he would procure the thing she needed (since he was a wealthy King, he feared the lands beyond his Kingdom). As the girl grew, the King became sad because he knew that one day, the child in question would soon leave him to her husband's house. His cause of worry was not that the girl would leave him but that she may never find another person who would love her as he did. He needed someone that would do anything to satisfy her just like he had always done.

The girl did not make it easy for her father, either; she was stunning to behold. Thus, she had many male admirers and suitors. The rich men in the Kingdom were all interested in her for their selfish reasons. Among those who expressed their desires to have her hand in marriage was a poor blacksmith. He had nothing to offer in exchange except his love, but he knew he would not give up without trying.

When the King felt that the time was ripe, he called together all the suitors. They all came in their fanciful dressings, bearing several delicacies and mouth-watering gifts for the King. The blacksmith came with nothing other than a high staff he had wrought especially for the King. It was not even coated in gold. When they had all gathered, the King announced that whoever would marry his daughter would have to embark on a journey to a place he would reveal to them later. He would go without the provision of water and food and must come back with evidence which would also be told to them later. He then dismissed them by asking them to go home and think about it. Anyone who was interested should come back the next day to declare his intentions. Everyone left after the King had given his speech.

The next day, early in the morning, the blacksmith hurried to the palace to inform the King of his decision. The King acknowledged him and asked him to wait to see if another person would like to join. From morning till night, they waited, but no one ever showed to indicate interest. In the night, the King gave the girl to the blacksmith in marriage. There was never a journey. It was all a plan to know who would do everything in his power to achieve the goal of getting the bride. Resilience makes the rich. The King further broke tradition by making the blacksmith the crowned Prince. The blacksmith was indeed happy. He took a step of action toward what he desired and got rewarded on an unimaginable level.

Resilience makes the rich.

An important lesson to be learned from this story is that a step taken to implement a goal is a step taken in making a dream come true! Goal implementation requires a person to take some actions that will give the venturer an opportunity to understand the reality of his work. The venturer can estimate the prospect of his work and conclude whether it would be worth the effort to be invested. The goal implementation stage will present a situation that will test both the strength and the weakness of a venturer. Since he has to confront the reality of his work, the venturer will be forced to fight any unavoidable issue that is associated with it. His ability to overcome the situation will automatically elevate him and draw prospects to the horizon. The experience will also earn him a sense of assurance that he can achieve better success with more investment of effort.

A venturer must give whatever it takes to execute his plan once he can perceive success is within his grasp. The roadmap may wind up becoming more challenging than anticipated, because some unforeseen circumstances arise. Plans may fall short of perfection. Resources may be inadequate, and other unprecedented issues may arise. The venturer must continue to take the journey until he can meet his target goal. A venturer must not hesitate to seek a solution for his problem no matter the type and the magnitude. He cannot afford to allow his negative circumstances to ground his efforts and derail his success-intended journey. The person must resist his opposition and remove any obstacle on his path to actualize his plan and roll toward meeting his success target.

Goal implementation requires a person to take some actions that will give the venturer an opportunity to understand the reality of his work.

Despite the fact that a venturer has an obligation to follow through with his dream and bring it to a stage of practical implementation, he still has the choice to either take an immediate action or schedule the process for a future date. If he decides to postpone the process, he must be disciplined enough to ensure that it is carried out at the slated date and time. If, for any reason, he continues to postpone the goal implementation, he may end up becoming discouraged and ultimately dump the whole ambition. Regrettably, this will result in a waste of all resources invested.

Once a decision is reached to embark on goal implementation, a venturer can choose to gradually implement his plan before any major full-scale implementation. He may do this to avoid making any significant error that can affect his overall efforts. The gradual rollout process can also grant him an opportunity to learn from minor mistakes. However, the system of gradual implementation must not be overstretched; you want to avoid losing the momentum needed to drive the work to a completion.

Challenges of Goal Implementation

A wealthy man was once asked by his neighbors how he continued to make it despite all odds. He told them he had his answer, but he would show it to them instead of telling them. He asked them to nominate three people among them. He further asked them to gather a large group of people as spectators. The next day, when they were all gathered, he gave each of the nominees a task. Each person was to carry an egg using a spoon from point A to B, which was a short distance. He went further to split the crowd into two groups. On one side stood the opposition party and the hailers stood on the other. The two parties were to either praise the nominees or jeer at them. Anyone who completed the task would take a gift at point B.

Only one of the contestants got to the destination and got the reward. When asked how he could do that amidst the noise, he owned up to tuning them out of his mind and ears. He chose not to consider them, let alone listen to them. For the other two, they had listened to the crowd. While one got demoralized by those mocking and hurling insults at him, the other got carried away by his progress and the praise. They learned how the man continued to grow; he neither listened to the admirers nor the mockers. He maintained focus on his goal at all times.

No one likes an obstacle, but unfortunately, a few barriers are bound to confront a venturer as he aims to implement his goal plan. He may soon realize that some parts of his plan won't work due to unforeseen circumstances. He may be confronted with lack of resources. Sometimes, he may get distracted, or he may face other unprecedented situations. Whatever the kind of obstacle encountered, the venturer must be determined to overcome it and continue to implement his plan to meet the overall project target.

The stage of goal implementation offers a venturer an opportunity to have a practical understanding of his work better than what he had envisaged during the planning stage. The person will face the reality of his work to make accurate decisions. He may see the need to rearrange his goal plan to meet a newly developed situation. He may also see the need to completely change a goal plan that he considers to be non-prospective.

A venturer must be sensitive to remove the distractions from his work during the implementation stage. Distracting activities will pop up left and right. The venturer must ensure that he does not allow any of them to slow down the progress of his work. The person must make an excellent effort to eliminate those activities as much as possible. He should aim to limit

> *A venturer must be sensitive to remove the distractions from his work during the implementation*

their influences if he concludes they can't be eliminated. Once they have been reduced or eliminated, the venturer must seize the opportunity to create a positive environment for himself. Based on personal preferences, he may post an inspirational quote to a conspicuous location of his work environment. He may plant flowers, drop background curtains or hang pictures of his motivating legends on the wall. Whatever option he adopts, the person must keep in mind that he has no other choice than to maintain the momentum to achieve the overall success he anticipates.

Motivation in Quest for Success

The word *motivation* is often described as the main contributor to success. However, the description is overstretched, since motivation alone does not amount to success. Motivation can contribute to success, but it is not the only ingredient needed. Motivation misses some essential elements that lead to success generation. For example, a typical motivation does not have a specific plan that someone can follow to achieve his goal. Motivation, in most cases, does not provide an answer to the question of what, when, where and how a target can be actualized. Anyone who mainly depends on motivation to achieve his goal may soon realize he or she is not making enough effort. The person may have his mind geared toward his aspiration, but he still needs to engage his work with a workable goal plan.

A person who relies solely on motivation to drive his goal runs the risk of exposing himself to a roller-coaster emotional experience. His mind will be tossed up and down, as he can be very productive when motivated, but be less productive in the absence of motivation. The emotional ride will eventually throw him off balance toward inadequate overall performance.

However, a person who works with a specific plan to run a project will have the odds of mood swings thrown into the garbage, since the plan will *become* his motivation. The person can remain productive in the absence of extrinsic "motivation." He can maintain momentum to perform at a full threshold on a consistent basis. The specificity of his action plan will also help him to prepare his mind to make the best use of any resources available.

Someone who depends on a specific goal plan to operate his task (against depending on motivation to drive him) can have a smooth run of his work from the beginning to the end without suffering from any unnecessary emotional hiccups. The consistency of his operation style will earn him a sense of assurance that he is making meaningful progress that can lead to achieving the overall success anticipated.

Security Consciousness

Security is vital to every venture; a prospective venturer must provide security for his work. An absence of good protection may cause the person to suffer the loss of his investment. Theft and any form of accident can lead to a security breach. Also, in this digital age, any computer-related work can be abruptly lost due to a hard drive problem. The device may crash, become infected, or affected in othdr ways to cause significant data damage. Storage devices can become corrupted and render data inaccessible. Worse still, a cyber-attack can cause a user's data to disappear overnight. In short, any slight adverse occurrence can result in a significant data loss. A person whose work is digitally related must venture to have antivirus protection for his computing device. He should also backup his jobs to a secured location.

An absence of good protection may cause a person to suffer the loss of his investment.

A person who does an excellent job of backing up his work will have something to salvage should an unforeseen issue occur. A good backup system must incorporate the most recent duplicate of ongoing work. It must contain the version that can be safely recalled and must have current activities that are being performed. It will help the adventurer to quickly regain momentum and avoid repeating a task that he had completed.

A good backup exercise must be done on a routine basis and be performed according to a schedule. It can be a recurrent hourly,

134

weekly, monthly, or yearly event. The task can be performed manually or automatically. Fortunately, recent technology has provided an opportunity that anyone can explore to set up automatic backup synchronization to local or cloud-based devices. A prospective adventurer should consider the two options since they have slightly different benefits.

Meanwhile, beyond the importance of any data storage, a prospective venturer must have backup plans for his work. He must have Plan A, B, and C ready to salvage his work in case an unavoidable security breach or job loss occurs. That is, the person must have Plan B launch-ready to replace Plan A in case of a failure. He must also have Plan C intact should Plan A and Plan B fail under whatever circumstance.

Key Points

➢ Planning without action is an effort in futility. After the necessary goal planning, there must be an implementation.

➢ The implementation stage is when true strength will be tested and weaknesses will be exposed. It is when the real test of a plan occurs.

➢ Anybody who can recognize the prospect in a project will not cease to persevere.

➢ The eye of the venturer should be on the goal and not focused on the noise and distractions around him.

➢ Goal implementation may be immediate or delayed. However, when it is suspended, a venturer must be disciplined enough to ensure that it is diligently executed on a picked date.

➤ Challenges are like milestones on the way to success. Therefore, there can be no success without challenges.

➤ You must do everything in your power to overcome obstacles, or they will limit you.

➤ Time management is a skill to be acquired if success must be attained.

➤ Motivation alone is not enough for success. Motivation, coupled with a specific goal, on the other hand, will give excellent results.

➤ Develop your skills and update yourself from time to time. Nothing ever remains the same, as change is constant.

➤ Make your work secure.

EDUCATION IS SUCCESS'S RELATIVE

The whole purpose of education is to turn mirrors into windows.

Sydney J. Harris

Bill Gates was in his second year at Harvard when he dropped out of school. This is popularly propagated by those who do not like to go to school and do not want to be bothered. However, that is not the right way to look at it. Gates was in his second year at Harvard when he took a *leave of absence*. He left it open so that he could always return to school in case he failed at the business setup. However, he did not, because he never planned to and did not have to go back to school. The person that succeeded him as CEO, Steve Ballmer, was a magnum cum laude graduate of Harvard. Education helped Gates, and he used the proceeds from the Mothers' club to purchase a computer for the students, which he later programmed. He was excused from math class to go after what he wanted to do. Several decades after he left school, Gates has and is pumping enough resources into the educational sector, because he knows just how vital it is.

> *Any society that prioritizes education is bound to thrive!*

Education has been a relative to success from time immemorial. It will also remain an essential tool for success in this present age.

Any society that prioritizes education is bound to thrive! Also, a parent who ventures to obtain a good education for his child will increase his chance of becoming successful in life. People who value education go out of their way to acquire it. For the sake of its benefit, some countries annually budget billions of dollars to fund their education system. Some parents also heavily invest in the education of their children. Parents who value education but can't afford it obtain loans.

If someone asks, "Why is education so important?" the answer is that it is a formidable tool of progress. Education brings prospects to people and also increases the wealth of a society. A person that has a good education has a good chance of becoming successful in life.

Education has a lot of benefits to offer: It enhances a person's opportunity to have a better future than he would have without its platform. It helps a person to develop successful habits. A person who has an education is likely to have creative ability to solve problems and create an alternate path for the ones he can't solve. An educated person can intuitively envision a problem and devise a solution or it. He can also adapt to any new situation and thrive in it.

Education is indeed vital to every aspect of human life. No person in his right mind should claim he has a substitute for a good education. Even folks who claim to be born-geniuses still need an education to make the best use of their minds.

Education has two categories, which are formal education and informal education. Formal education has a specific curriculum that covers some particular areas of study that put the learner's ability into consideration. Formal education is often supervised by a relevant professional board, which enforces discipline with specific rules.

Typical informal education does not have any curriculum in place to help both the teacher and student operate under specific board rules. Informal education can be obtained from various sources. The teaching of parents and other loved ones can be categorized as informal education. A social organization can also be a source of informal education. A person who receives informal education has the responsibility to vet it before any application. Since any official body does not supervise the process, the teacher is prone to teach on a random basis. He is most likely to teach his areas of interest while he lays little emphasis on others, or completely ignores them. Also, since the teacher may not have the proper assessment tools, the student may end up learning in a relaxed environment and miss the opportunity of being exposed to academic challenges. These limitations will eventually make the scale imbalanced, and the system becomes offset.

A prospective venturer must aspire to have as much formal education as possible. If he has an elementary or a high school education, he should also step up his efforts to acquire a college education. If he has the opportunity, he should obtain a graduate education to boost his success skills. A person who for any reason could not obtain a formal education should make good use of any informal education he can get. His effort to adequately educate himself will eventually pay off.

Anyone who wants to succeed in life must make education his priority. He has no substitute for good education if he wants to succeed. The person cannot sit around to blame the government for not helping enough to make education affordable. The person

Anyone who wants to succeed in life must make education his priority.

cannot blame his relatives, either. He should make an excellent effort to help himself if no one is ready to help him. He may have to do some research by walking up to some schools to make admission inquiries. If he lacks funds, he may have to do some menial labor to gather money. The person also has a choice to seek assistance from charity organizations. There is always someone or some organization out there that can help him. If, under whatever circumstance, the person cannot receive financial help from sources he consults, he should venture to borrow money for his education. He should research a low-interest student loan that can serve the purpose of obtaining a good education.

Key Points

➢ Education is key to success.

➢ The continued existence of any society is based on how much they spend on educating the upcoming generation.

➢ Education may not assure you of success, but it provides you a platform or foundation for success.

➢ Both formal and informal types of education should be acquired for balance; the two arms are needed for the development of a well-rounded individual.

THE APPLICATION
OF EDUCATION

*Education is not the learning of facts, but the
training of the mind to think.*

Albert Einstein

Tom is a graduate of Engineering. He finished with distinction but has been unable to get a job ever since he left the university. While he was in school, he would devote time to poring over his books, cramming as much as he could into his brain. Often, he would not remember anything after an examination, but he was not bothered. His scores were excellent, and his GPA kept rising. As long as he had that, he had no cause for worry. He only had to present his certificate, and he would get a job.

How wrong he was! Now, three years have gone by, and he has been unable to secure a job. Even his colleagues that did not have the excellent grades he had are doing fine. While he was busy chasing after the scores, they sought not just the knowledge, but the understanding of what they were taught. That was the difference between them. The certificate was useless without the ability to demonstrate what he knew.

No one will ask a physicist to state the Laws of Motion, neither will a doctor be told to name all the diseases that have been discovered. However, the physicist will be expected to make an informed decision and proffer a solution if an instrument acts weird. The doctor will be required to make a prognosis based on the presentation of signs and symptoms. None of them will be expected to go back to their notebooks or textbooks to find solutions to all questions. If they have to search through the notes again, it will be to update themselves or refresh their memories.

A person who has a good education is also expected to have the ability to thrive in his field of operation. Life after school is entirely different, and he must be able to make his education relevant to real-life situations. Besides, every job out there is characteristically unique, which will require that an educated person can adapt his book knowledge to meet its needs. Someone who is educated is expected to outperform someone else who has a lesser level of education (or does not have any form of exposure). An educated person is expected to have the ability to thrive in any operational environment.

> *A person who has a good education is also expected to have the ability to thrive in his field of operation.*

Every aspect of education is useful for success generation. However, some jobs require specialized education. A prospective person ought to subscribe to the educational type that will improve his status. However, basic education is always relevant and applicable to all kinds of jobs. Basic education applies to all fields and can be a good starting point for anyone who finds himself in a field that is not related to his education background. He can get his operation off the ground pending the time that he can obtain any applicable specialized education he needs.

An advanced form of education is most relevant to professions that require some level of expertise. A person whose job falls into this category ought to make every effort to acquire the specific

142

education that will help him to become adequately productive. Of course, as earlier mentioned, he can take advantage of his primary education to keep the ball rolling while he tries to acquire any special education he needs.

The fact remains that not everyone will find a job in an area that is directly related to his educational background. A person's ability to adapt any education he has to an unfamiliar field of operation will be considered as a show of his strength. However, this assertion does not apply to every situation. Someone does not have to endure a distasteful job for the sake of satisfying an ego, or for any other reason. If the person has a solid alternative, he should go for it. He ought to explore any prospective opportunity that can help him achieve premium success. Better still, if there are enough resources, a person who dislikes a job can start his own business that will grant

> *A person's ability to adapt any education he has to an unfamiliar field of operation will be considered as a show of his strength.*

him the flexibility to suitably apply his education and skills to meet his success expectations.

Key Points

➢ The essence of education is for you to be able to apply it to problems and bring solutions or positive changes.

➢ All things being equal, anyone who has enjoyed education should perform well at his job.

- ➤ While some jobs require advanced education due to the level of expertise needed for such professions, the basic level would suffice for some others.
- ➤ There should be a distinction between an educated fellow and someone who has never stepped on the shores of one.
- ➤ Having one form of education or the other does not mean you cannot go into business.
- ➤ Do not degrade yourself.

THE IMPORTANCE OF RESEARCH

I believe in innovation and that the way you get innovation is you fund research and you learn the basic facts.

Bill Gates

Research and Education

"Sow your seed in the morning, and at evening let your hands not be idle, for you do not know which will succeed, whether this or that, or whether both will do equally well." (Ecclesiastes 11:6 - NIV)

The Motorola Company name was on everybody's lips not too long ago, but where are they today? In 2014, the company eventually split up and, like the way a cooked turkey is shared at dinner, limbs of the establishment got divided. The company started as a family affair in 1928. Through the years, power changed hands and innovations were made. Motorola thrived as it had no significant competition. In 1997, Nokia surpassed Motorola and took over the market for approximately the next fifteen years by going the extra mile to upgrade to digital phones. Motorola had worked primarily on cellular and wireless devices.

With a well-calculated and simultaneously desperate move, Chris Galvin, a grandson of the founder, Paul, thought of the Razr, a slim, metallic phone that went on to turn the declining fortune of the company around. Chris only heard of this success because he had been shown the way out. With a new CEO, Zander, and several bad decisions and lack of research, the days of the Razr soon phased out, leaving the company in a ditch. Several

> *Anyone who fails to research and improve the quality of his work will soon be pushed out of the limelight.*

attempts were made at different times to resuscitate the company, including the creation of the Droid after separation, but the situation was too dire. The inevitable was imminent.

A success-aspiring person must be inclined to do research that can improve his products and services. His research must not only focus on raising the profit margin, but it must include the need to enhance the quality of life. That is, proper research must solve people's specific problems. It must also at least raise awareness about one so that someone else can pick up the challenge to address it. Anyone who fails to research and improve the quality of his work will soon be pushed out of the limelight. People will look for an alternative product that can better serve them and also meet any new problem they face. In short, the lack of formidable research can fail any business.

The need for research is to benefit an enterprise and also improve the quality of life, which cannot be overemphasized. Research brings prospect to an endeavor. It leads to innovation and earns improvement opportunities for an existing effort. Folks in the business

> *Research brings prospect to an endeavor.*

cycle understand the importance of research. They make it a priority to keep evaluating their work and make it relevant (It's a SMART thing to do!).

Research has contributed to the advancement of the world system. Some amenities that people enjoy today are the products of research that previous generations conducted. People who are inclined to research continue to improve the facilities and make them more efficient. They make innovations of their studies to earn benefits and improve people's lives. Telecommunication and transportation systems are excellent references, here. The two systems once had limited services to offer people, but their uses have been taken to a new level. People don't hang around telephone booths to make phone calls anymore. They now have the opportunity to own portable devices that can receive calls through transmission towers across the world!

Transportation systems have seen significant improvement in our day as people continue to research how they can improve the quality of lives. Mounting on horseback and riding in carts are no longer primary means of transportation. Also, a bicycle is no longer considered attractive to the majority of people. Recent research has not only unveiled the invention of cars, but people have also added much comfort to their value. People can now enjoy riding their vehicles with the sense of security features that new-generation cars have.

Meanwhile, not only has the transportation system improved on land, but it has also improved in water and air. Various researchers have brought both water and air transportation to new levels that allow people to sail in cruise ships without being restricted by traffic lights and speed radar. Perhaps that won't be exciting enough when compared with the fantastic benefits of air transportation. Aircraft of different shapes and sizes showcase the fruit of researchers' efforts.

Not only can airplanes transport a person through a long distance within a short time, but more advanced crafts can go far beyond the Earth's atmosphere to touch down on the moon and other planets. What amazing privileges research efforts have brought to the world transportation system!

The existence of internet has made research work a smooth exercise for success admirers. This amenity has virtually influenced almost all types of businesses since it has become available for public usage. Researchers use the platform to explore an opportunity to improve their products and meet people's needs. Every prospective entrepreneur ought to consider the benefit of the internet for his business, rather than being complacent with any status quo.

To cap it all, every prospective venturer must understand how research is relevant to his business. He can't pick a research topic at random and expect it to lead to success. The person must focus on research that will be relative to his products. That is, any research effort that a venturer makes must help his products and services become more relevant in the marketplace.

Any research effort that a venturer makes must help his products and services become more relevant in the marketplace.

A person who fails to perform research that can help him respond to market needs will see his lucrative business kicked out in a short time. Competitors will fill the vacuum and create wealth for themselves. He will lose whatever edge he had over them. Also, since customers often change their tastes to follow the trend of innovation, they will declare any existing product obsolete in a short while. They will always be willing to grasp any newly improved product that can satisfy their never-ending desires.

A lack of formidable research has dearly cost some recently successful businesses significant setbacks. They lost their competitive advantage and eventually became bankrupt. Against the popular opinion, those companies did not fail because of funds mismanagement. They failed because their leaders did not conduct research and improve their products to keep them more relevant. Their nonchalant attitude to research severed them from an opportunity to make the innovation that could help them adapt to an ever-changing business terrain. They eventually became out of touch with reality as they were forced out of success loop. However, while the situation remains unfortunate for some folks, others quickly fill the vacuum and take the advantage of the situation. This becomes evident as some little-known businesses rapidly come into the limelight and thrive. They soon became multi-billion-dollar establishments merely

> *Against the popular opinion, those companies that went bankrupt did not fail because of funds mismanagement. They failed because their leaders did not conduct research and improve their products to keep them more relevant.*

because they engaged in research. Their leaders were in tune with reality to know what people needed. They researched to meet the need, and they became successful. A good example of this is the Amazon website that Jeff Bezos started in the garage of his house with a focus to sell used books. The continuous researches and improvements Bezos conducted and his theme have turned the website to a giant search engine that now features multiple products with billions of dollars in profits.

149

Whether you take it or leave it, the size of an organization contributes to the rate of its success and failure. Leaders of small organizations can effect changes. They can maneuver around odds more easily than big corporations that may be beset with incessant bureaucracy. However, irrespective of the size of an organization, and whether it has failed in the past or not, formidable research can positively turn the dynamics of its status. Should the establishment fail to respond to the need of conducting necessary research to improve its products (and services), it will suffer a major setback and eventually become an history. It will fail!

> *Whether you take it or leave it, the size of an organization contributes to the rate of its success and failure.*

Research in the Quest for Invention

Viable research must generate an invention that would target a particular problem and reward the venturer who invested his resources. The person involved must ensure to keep focus and meet his or her goal of making his effort rewarding and be beneficial for the use of others. However, not all people fall in love with innovation. Only a few folks of the professed invention lovers are ready to invest their efforts. Folks who avoid change believe the process would be

> *Viable research must generate an invention that would target a particular problem and reward the venturer who invested his resources.*

counterproductive should it fail to meet an anticipated goal. They are afraid of risking their valuable resources should the innovation fail. Therefore, they decide to maintain a firm stand with the status quo.

However, courageous people work their way up the ladder of success with innovations. They choose not to allow anxiety of change consume them. They are less bothered with the perspiration of *Where and How* and do what it takes to get the resources they need. One step at a time, they seek and find answers to each of their questions and maintain the focus to pursue innovation for the sake of raising their intrinsic value. These folks understand that the prospect of their work is tied to a new invention or technique. Therefore, they are willing to explore every opportunity that can help them achieve their purpose.

Truly, innovation can be demanding and requires a person to go out of his way most of the time. A person who attempts to try innovation will have a few questions run through his mind, which he must answer to be successful. However, if the person has too many unknowns or lacks valid answers for most of his questions, he is more or less gambling. Too many unknowns will jeopardize his efforts.

An aspiring innovator must properly evaluate the activities that may be involved in his work as well as consider any risk that may be associated with it. His evaluation may mean a need to revise his plan or completely stop it. If he shuns every warning and makes an irrational decision to pursue the exercise, the effort will likely fail. A success-minded innovator must allow the following steps to guide him into making the proper preparation before embarking on his innovation:

1. Investigate to have adequate knowledge

A venturer must investigate any field he selects for innovation. He must have a good understanding of the field to have his work make a meaningful impact on it. If the person realizes he has insufficient knowledge in the area, he should bend to learn more or withdraw the effort. He should also stop any innovation that he understands will not make a meaningful effect on the targeted field. However, the innovator can proceed with his effort if the primary goal is to provide a temporary solution. His effort may provide material support for someone who will pick up the tab on the

It is important that an adventurer devotes his resources of time, money, and energy into an innovation that he believes can reward him in the end.

project.

It is important that an adventurer devotes his resources of time, money, and energy into an innovation that he believes can reward him in the end.

2. Communicate with the experts

Indeed, nothing is new under heaven. No matter how unique a research effort may sound, someone somewhere has already thought about it or has done something related to it. A person who intends to innovate ought to consult with the individuals with a related background to obtain useful information from them. He will learn from their experiences and turn them into material information needed to avoid mistakes and adequately channel his course into achieving his goal. However, it is important to note that most intelligent people are always willing to share their experience with other associates who can take their operational field to a new level of higher achievement.

3. Think about the cost of innovation

Money is needed to implement creativity of any type or size! The price involved may be a few thousand dollars, and it may sometimes rise to millions and billions of dollars. It is therefore essential that a venturer evaluates the cost involved in his innovation before he starts to embark on it. If he fails to estimate the rate carefully, he may end up building a bridge that leads to nowhere. That is, his innovative effort may hang in-between implementation and finish line. A person who wants his creative attempts to run smoothly from start to finish must make a wise decision first to raise adequate funds for it.

Research and innovation can be costly. However, the rule of thumb is that an innovator does not spend all his fortune on a discovery until he is utterly confident that it will yield him a good result. Innovation is all about testing new ground; no matter how sure it appears, something can go wrong. Therefore, the person involved must minimize his expenses as much as possible. An intuitive innovator will first make a beta product and subject it to thorough practical operation before embarking on a large-scale exercise. Even when his effort is declared successful, the person is still expected to gradually raise the production rate as he continues to monitor the performances and listen to customers' feedback.

Not all innovations are successful. While some lead to success, others don't. However, whether an invention passes or fails on the testing ground, the spirit of an invention doesn't die. The innovator would have learned one lesson or the other that he can use in his next trial. There is no better virtue than practical experience. Every innovator will have an opportunity to learn from his efforts, which will become an experience that makes him an inch closer to achieving success in his next trial. His experience is an asset that will earn him the opportunity to envision a problem, replicate it, troubleshoot it, and solve it. Perhaps the best advantage of innovation, whether successful or not, is the fact that an innovator will increase his stamina to withstand any future challenge that may arise. He will have the ability to handle any

> *Not all innovations are successful. While some lead to success, others don't. However, whether an invention passes or fails on the testing ground, the spirit of an invention doesn't die. The innovator would have learned one lesson or the other that he can use in his next trial. There is no better virtue than practical experience.*

similar project in the future successfully.

Key Points

➢ Research drives success. It is in the heart of success itself.

➢ If there is no product innovation and upgrade, consumers will soon grow tired.

➢ Any research engaged in should meaningfully contribute to the business or area of interest. Random research has no value to anyone.

➢ Although the size of an establishment may be inversely proportional to the speed of effecting change, no organization can resist the positive impacts of research.

➢ Any research undertaken should lead to an invention or innovation and not just conducted for the fun of it.

➢ There are several items the investigator should bear in mind between the conduction of the research and launching of innovation. They include:

- Investigate to have proper knowledge
- Think about the cost of innovation
- Communicate with the experts

➢ Not all innovations are successful. Brace yourself for some down moments. Failure is not necessarily the opposite of success. How you handle it will determine the outcome. It is a part of the success story.

WHAT FOLLOWS AFTER THE RUBBER MEETS THE ROAD?

The time will come when diligent research over long periods will bring to light things which now lie hidden.

Seneca

Remember the story of the Motorola Razr? How the slim cell phone came to save the day? For two years, Zander, the CEO of the company at that time rode on the wings of the innovation made by his predecessor. However, he did nothing to improve on it. Whatever changes effected were superficial. Change in color, packaging, et cetera, but nothing about the software or that could directly hold the interest of the consumer. The quality remained static. Finally, the people got bored and went with the new wave of innovation. So, what should be done when an innovation has been made and is accepted? What should be the next line of action for a researcher, innovator or a venturer? The thing is, a venturer will have some rewards to count on once his rubber meets the road. He will have a product to display and some benefits earned, which he can choose to either consume or preserve. In most cases, the venturer will be better off delaying the consumption of the spoils of his first round of achievement, because more opportunities may follow suit, which can become an added advantage to raise his success scale.

A person who has labored to bring his work to a finished state must also strive to add quality to it, or to move to the next innovation. The need to maintain and improve quality must remain his focus. Do we have the iPhone alone, or the improved 2, 3 ,4, 5, 6, 7, 8, 10, and S series? Continuous improvement will help to create lasting impressions on the consumers' minds. Once he can gain their confidence, they will gravitate to his brand and are most likely to keep patronizing any other product that he may have in the future. However, should the person pay less attention to quality, customers will seek a better alternative that meets their expectations.

A venturer will be pressured to trade quality for quantity as his work becomes more acceptable in the market. He will see the need to conserve his limited resources and mass produce his product at the same time. It will tempt him to reduce the quality of his

> *A person who has labored to bring his work to a finished state must also strive to add quality to it, or to move to the next innovation.*

product. However, should the person fall into this trap, he will lose product credibility. Consumers will lose interest and look for a viable alternative, and this will affect his overall success. If the person fails to take appropriate remedial action on time, the situation may cause him to lose the business altogether.

An old saying, *"first impressions last longer"* is true and still relevant today. A venturer who has invested so much effort to bring his work to a stable state ought to also endure any remaining stress needed to polish it with every necessary detail to make it the best of its kind. He must enforce quality assurance during and after the implementation stage. That is, the work must be properly examined before declaring it completed, and before sending out any press releases about it.

Meanwhile, it is not just the quality of a product a venturer must pursue; he must also make his own life be of high quality! The quality of his life will reflect on his work. To achieve this feat, the person must continuously expose himself to related information and training. More training will not hurt but only benefit a person. They will add extra value to his life to become more prosperous. Regular academic arena, trade school, public library, and internet learning can be good sources of information and training. Soak up information wherever you can find it, but make sure your sources are reliable.

Prospective information and training will help an adventurer become a person with a better career irrespective of his profession and field of operation. A success-conscious person must aspire to learn more and grow. For example, a musician who is comfortable in playing one note can train to improve on playing others. A singer can train to improvise and raise his pitch to sing on the next scale. A businessperson can improve his interpersonal skills. The list of the benefits to earn from information and training to generate quality success goes on and on.

The Morality of a Successful Person

A person's character will come to full display once the rubber meets the road and things start to go well for him or her. His true colors will be on display as his investment yields profit, and people begin to notice him. The person has the choice to appreciate God and the people who offered him support along the way. He can also choose to be puffed up and ungrateful to people who lent him helping hands. The person can also choose to shun his old friends and pick up a few elites in replacement. However, the best choice is for the person to be responsible and appreciative of his success to everyone who helped him. Should he choose to be ungrateful, he will lose the privilege of receiving future help.

> *A person's character will come to full display once the rubber meets the road and things start to go well for him or her.*

Someone who has become successful ought to be insightful and understand the mysteries that surround his achievement. Success rides on roller coasters; it has no permanent destination. It may camp with someone today and decamp tomorrow. A circumstance of life can influence the success of any magnitude. Not even a skilled person can permanently keep success at his beck and call; the situations of life can change his status.

A person who has become successful can see the reversal of his wealth, as the cause may be a market crash, health crisis, poor personal decision, and disappointment from an associate, or any other circumstance. The unfortunate situation may cause the person who had flown in his private jet and shook hands with prominent people around the world to become an everyday man or woman who has no exclusive authority.

Every successful person ought to find a balance in his approach to life. A person must ensure his desires for success do not lead him to lose his human dignity. He must endeavor to be humane and add the virtue of morality to his life. A successful person ought to be responsible and compassionate in his dealings with people and businesses. He must also see the need to make himself a source of positive influence on the people with whom he interacts.

Unfortunately, some successful people fail the character test, even though they have successful businesses. They fall into the Grade F category when assessed for interpersonal skills. They focus on their ambitions and become blindsided to other aspects of life, which are also important. Folks in this category allow their wealth obsession to cancel their personal dignity. They let their wealth control them when they should entertain the opposite.

Obsessed folks rarely have a settled mind; they consistently have mood swings. They can be happy in the morning, sad in the afternoon, and miserable at night. Something always comes up that will make them lose their joy,

> *Obsessed folks rarely have a settled mind; they consistently have mood swings.*

which may be a failed business, a missed contract, or a low profit. These folks are unsatisfied and prone to comparing themselves with other people. They would be willing to rule the world for their wealth. However, once the reality of their wealth hunt becomes evident, they often slip into using drugs and pursue other immoral conduct that eventually derails their success journey.

The Principles of a Successful Person

A person who has seen his dream come true ought to be careful not to allow it to control him. He ought to be in control of his wealth and not let the reverse happen. Once his rubber meets the road, he should discipline himself to know the difference between living a responsible lifestyle and an irresponsible one. The person must be accountable for himself, his family and his society. He must keep a good moral standard and be a source of positive influence to others.

> *A person who has seen his dream come true ought to be careful not to allow it to control him.*

The person who has worked hard to earn his success ought to enjoy his wealth. He should treat himself well as a reward for his labor. However, the person ought to be careful not to abuse the privilege of rewarding himself by turning it into a basis for living a wasteful lifestyle. He has no reason to flaunt his wealth for ego satisfaction, and neither does he need to spend a dime to impress someone. The person ought to have integrity and be guided by a few self-imposed rules to maintain a good moral standard.

Success has no limit. Someone who has become successful will desire to have more. Meanwhile, the person ought to be careful not to be obsessed with desire for wealth accumulation and lose his human dignity in the process. While the person makes an effort to raise his success scale, he must be humane enough to care and spend on other people. He should care for people who are less privileged and allow his wealth to trickle onto them. He must consider it necessary to take part in humanitarian work. Plenty of charity needs are out there that he can support. Many poor people live in the same world with him. Considerable percentages of the world population are living under one dollar a day; the majority of them cannot afford three square meals a day. This reason alone should be enough motivation for a successful person to help!

Reasonable successful people are not misers. They are not possessive of their wealth, but they share with others. Some people are more fortunate than others, so they lend helping hands to the underprivileged. These folks consider it helpful to sponsor the provision of essential amenities for the poor community. They invest in poor neighborhoods to create jobs for the unemployed. They offer scholarships for underprivileged children. They build schools, roads, and hospitals to help improve people's quality of lives. These reasonable people are passionate to fund research programs that can cure terminal diseases.

Meanwhile, it is not just the significantly rich who can care for other people. Some so-called minimally successful people are also responsible and caring. They refused to allow their needs to become successful stop them from sparing a few resources to cater to other people who are desperately in need.

Key Points

➢ After the product has been made, the next pursuit should be the maintenance of quality.

➢ People will always choose quality over quantity. Once you can assure them of your unwavering devotion to quality, they will keep coming to you.

162

➢ Invest heavily in training, because it can never amount to waste.

➢ Whatever impression people first have of you will go a long way in determining how they will relate to you in the long run. A first impression is often said to last longer if not forever. For it to change, extra effort will have to be employed.

➢ Nothing exposes the true colors of a man more than success and money. Develop your personality so that it does not stand in your way later.

➢ Treat everyone well when you have attained the coveted success, especially those who lend you a hand.

➢ You should always be in control. Do not let the success go to your head.

➢ The more wealth you have, the more you will crave. Be disciplined enough not to get obsessed with the pursuit of money and accumulation of riches. Nobody takes anything along when they are dead.

➢ Use your success and wealth to help others.

➢ Do not be a miser; enough people need your assistance.

CONCLUSION

STRAIGHT TALK TO YOU!

As a person whose goal is to achieve tangible life success, you must do whatever is necessary to add quality to your work. Anything worth doing at all is worth doing well. Do your best by all standards to raise your success scale. Invest in education to improve your morale. Be your own source of motivation. Don't wait for someone else to motivate you but push yourself forward toward achieving your success goal. Make out-of-pocket expenses to invest in activities that can increase your intrinsic value. Sign up for necessary classes to obtain useful information for your career advancement. Also, take certificate courses, get licenses, and attend seminars.

Refuse to be complacent with the status quo. Mediocrity goes nowhere, but *you,* an aspirant of success, must break free from every limiting factor. Engage actively in research to improve your quality and standards. Visit the library, subscribe to relevant magazines, and read useful articles on the internet. Never stop investing in your career until you have finally taken control of it to have sustained success.

As a success-aspiring person, you must take the journey of an *extra mile.*

The road to an extra mile is never crowded, but you have to choose to plough through it. Be determined not to feel lonely, as you may realize that only a few people are interested in taking the journey. Don't stop where others have stopped but choose to be defiant to every obstruction and push your way through into success.

As someone who is determined to succeed, you cannot afford to emulate people who have little or no aspiration for success. You must consider yourself a unique person who is ready to go far and beyond to achieve greatness. Even if you feel your cake is well baked, you should still consider it necessary to take the journey of an extra mile to add some icing to it. Your efforts will make you stand out from the crowd and be esteemed as a successful person.

As a success-minded person, never consider an effort to detail your work with quality as a waste of time. Be excellent in whatever you do to leave a lasting impression on people's minds. Your extra effort will make consumers prefer you to other competitors. Even if they have sworn allegiance to someone else before meeting you, they will soon change their minds to become your longtime allies.

Quality must be your prime objective as a success-conscious person. Never compromise on it. Meanwhile, not everyone appreciates class, but a few individuals who know its worth will be willing to pay for it. They will pay any high price tag since they understand the long-term benefits they will derive from it. For example, an artist who went an extra mile to detail his artwork for a perfect illustration may not be appreciated by a clueless person who understands nothing about art, who may consider it as a chunk of ink on cardboard. Meanwhile, someone who knows the worth will be willing to sacrifice thousands of dollars to have it.

In addition to the artwork example, also consider the luxurious cars that some manufacturers specialize in making. The production line is scanty, but those manufacturers are thriving in business. Why? Their quality cars attract the affluent who have a taste for a quality machine! They are eager to pay the huge price for them. Not only that, they will keep coming back every few years to either trade or buy another brand new one.

It is vital that you, as a success-conscious person, relate with likeminded people and businesses to improve your experience. This principle has always been relevant to other aspects of life. It is also applicable to business. However, you must understand that everyone can't fall into your success circle. Choose a few folks and companies that share core values with you. Their practices may not be the same as yours, but they have to be relevant to some extent. Meanwhile, be careful not to bring every Tom, Dick and Harry to your prospect circle, because any wrong person can negatively influence it. Ensure that people and businesses you relate to are those who share common principles.

Success is not limited to business only. You must consider it necessary to extend the terrain of your success aspiration to other areas of life. You ought to care enough to keep your body healthy. You should also consider it essential to maintain the health of your relationships. Don't be trapped into a business pursuit and be subservient to other aspects of your life. Eat healthy food and exercise. Take time out of your busy schedule to spend quality time with people that matter to you. Go on vacation with your family and make them feel the warmness of your love.

Last but not least, never quit dreaming! Live every day of your life with at least one goal in mind to achieve. Besides resting periods and vacation time, never wake up on a day without having something in mind to achieve. Even at your retirement age, you must still be a dreamer. You may choose to spend the rest of your life on charity activities that won't take a toll on your health. Perhaps one of the most beneficial things someone can do when his rubber meets the road is to choose to be a channel of blessing to other people. You can choose the path of mentorship and share your experience with the generation of people that will take their world to a new level of achievement.

Do not just aspire to make a living, desire to make a difference!

AUTHOR'S NOTE

Success is what every one of us, myself included, wants to have in life. However, it seems no one, ironically, has successfully defined the term. As I went through the various literatures on the subject, I began to ponder what it really means for one to lay a claim to success. Is it about the fame, the inventions alone, the position in society or the money? Nothing seemed to satisfy me until I went on a trip of personal discovery. All I have learned is what I have written in here. Writing and teaching others about how to attain a successful life was more than meets the eye for me. It was one thing to know about the tenets of success, but it was quite another to put pen on paper to bring these tenets to you. It is my fervent hope that my words have inspired you and, through it all, I have no regrets for having aspired to that inspiration.

About Author

James Taiwo is the founder and senior pastor of World Outreach Evangelical Ministry. He holds a Doctor of Theology and a Master of Science in Environmental Engineering. He is the author of Bible Application Lessons and Prayers, the Book of Prayers, Bible Giants of Faith, Who Was Jesus Really?, Pinnacle of Compassion, Christian Principle Guides, and other books. He lives in New York City with his wife and children.

Add your honest, positive five stars review of this book online at

www.bit.ly/success-passcode

Visit the author's website.

www.jamestaiwo.com

Connect on social media

Facebook: facebook.com/jamestaiwoJT

Twitter: twitter.com/theJamesTaiwo

Amazon: amazon.com/author/jamestaiwo

www.ingramcontent.com/pod-product-compliance
Lightning Source LLC
Chambersburg PA
CBHW060028210326
41520CB00009B/1041